D1282864

MODERN AUSTRALIAN ABORIGINAL ART

MODERN AUSTRALIAN ABORIGINAL ART

By

REX BATTARBEE

ANGUS AND ROBERTSON

Sydney · London

Anglobooks

LONDON – NEW YORK – TORONTO

First American Edition 1952

First Published 1951

SET IN MONOTYPE TIMES ROMAN

PRINTED AND BOUND IN AUSTRALIA BY

HALSTEAD PRESS PTY LTD, NICKSON STREET, SYDNEY

REGISTERED IN AUSTRALIA FOR TRANSMISSION THROUGH THE POST AS A BOOK

CONTENTS

*

COLOURED PLATES

★

OTHER ILLUSTRATIONS

*

FOREWORD

*

SINCE the emergence of what may be termed without undue impropriety the "Hermannsburg School of Native Painting", there has been considerable controversy among artists and others about the present value and probable future of the work of full-blooded Australian aborigines who are expressing their ideas by means of European art techniques. Such discussions ultimately raise the question, "What was the nature and the purpose of the original form of art practised by the Australian natives?"

Before attempting to answer this query, I want to make it quite clear that I am not concerned with the questions, "What is Art?" or "Is Australian primitive art an expression of racial habits of thinking, genetically determined?" I am interested here only in the original purpose of native pictorial art and in the emotional and artistic appeal that it once made upon the aboriginal spectators. Since all the Hermannsburg artists discussed in this book are Aranda* men, I shall in this Foreword draw my illustrations and facts wholly from the pictorial productions of the Aranda tribe.

The original pictorial art of the Aranda will already be familiar to most readers. It consisted of painted decorations of shields and other weapons, of rock-drawings and rock-carvings, of ceremonial and totemic patterns executed on the persons of actors appearing in the sacred ceremonies or traditional dances associated with the various totems, and of incised designs on the sacred objects included in the Aranda term "tjurunga".† Aranda art was, therefore, intimately associated with utilitarian and sacred objects; and the ideas and scenes that it sought to set down were taken almost invariably from the sacred traditions of the tribe. The patterns themselves regularly employed such common geometric figures as circles, half-circles, spirals, and straight or curved lines; and to these were often added simple representations of the tracks of birds or animals. These figures were then combined into balanced patterns of greater or less elaborateness.

It should be stressed here that the completed patterns were never regarded as pieces of pure or abstract art by the natives themselves. All the figures I have just mentioned had always been used in everyday life by Aranda men, women, and children, who used to enjoy drawing them on smoothed-out sand whenever they

* Arunta.   † churunga.

[1

indulged in telling each other their stories or experiences. Thus, whereas a European looking at the incised pattern of a tjurunga would be thinking of it in terms of art and attempting to appreciate its lines, its drawing, its design, its composition, and so on, any Aranda native would have been conscious rather that a scene from a sacred story was lying open before his gaze. His reactions, therefore, would not have been unlike those of a European observer who is viewing a fine representational painting depicting a scene from mythology or history: the native's first reaction would have been joy at the artistry evident in the viewed object,* his second a keen desire to learn the full details of the scene depicted on the object.

In one important respect the Aranda man looking at his traditional patterns would have been at a considerable disadvantage when compared with the European looking at the picture of a mythical or historic scene. The latter would have shown the objects themselves, the former merely the figures or marks denoting the objects. To give an illustration: in ordinary sand-drawings, two half-circles on opposite sides of a central circle always denoted two human beings sitting (sometimes standing) on opposite sides of the central object in the scene depicted—a fire, a tree, a grindstone, a rock hole, or something similar. The *exact* interpretation of the central circle could be made clear only by the story-teller himself. Similarly, identical figures were used to denote kangaroo, euro, or wallaby tracks. The Aranda artist, therefore, could not tell his story wholly through his own special medium. Since his object was to tell a story, his art could only be called representational; but before his representation of the scene could be adequately appreciated, he had to receive help from a verbal description so as to make the intentions of his design clear beyond doubt to the spectators. The strongest emotional effect obtained by the Aranda artist was achieved in the figures painted or incised on his sacred ceremonial objects and in the patterns executed in blood and down, charcoal, pipeclay and ochres on the bodies of the actors in sacred ceremonies. For these were decorations celebrated in verse, and their emotional value depended largely on the knowledge by the initiated men of the chant verses referring to them. Thus, to give one example, in the Ilbalintja ceremonies the band around the waist of the actor and the two stripes descending upon it from his shoulders undoubtedly looked pleasing in themselves; but to the initiated men their effect was greatly strengthened by the interpretation given to this design in the appropriate chant verse—

> *The whirlwind is encircling his waist;*
> *Stripes fall down his back from his shoulders, and the whirlwind is encircling his waist.*

It is evident then that Aranda native art, though representational in its purpose, depended for its appeal in considerable measure upon the accompanying spoken word

* Mere artistic pleasure need not be very high when viewing a sacred object. A tjurunga which is very old and crudely decorated could easily, because of its age and significance, have moved the beholder to tears whereas a recently made and beautifully engraved object might have elicited no emotional response at all.

and chanted verse that made clear the purpose of the artist. The representational skill must, of course, not be unduly minimized. Aranda art showed a scene as viewed through the eyes of a native people whose whole existence had depended largely on their tracking ability. A Central Australian native used to read the ground like a book. If he came upon a deserted camp site, he could tell from looking at the earth how many men, women, and children had left their marks behind, where they had slept, where and what they had eaten, when they had last been there, and so on. The position of windbreaks and fires indicated to him facts about the presence of married couples and the number of husbandless women. Centuries of acute observation had similarly taught him to tell from tracks not only what kind of birds and animals were in his neighbourhood, but also what they had been doing before his arrival and what they were likely to be doing at the moment. As a result the Aranda people had, naturally enough, developed in their pictorial art the habit of looking down upon a landscape from above and not from the side, as we do. Even in the rare instances in which they sought to depict the trees, animals, or human beings themselves more or less "realistically", they viewed them from above—trees as circles with roots emanating from them, animals as dead creatures lying on their bellies with their legs stretched out on both sides, and human beings as recumbent figures reclining on their backs. But these "realistic" figures rarely—perhaps never—found their way into the decorations that had the highest emotional appeal, the sacred objects.

In spite of the severe limitations of their medium the Aranda artists were by no means lacking in inborn talent. Their works were, at their best, remarkable for their very high decorative quality, for the variety of the figure groupings introduced into them, and for the pleasing combinations of the four vivid colours almost exclusively used in them—white, black, red, and yellow. I have said earlier that in a sand-drawing a circle could denote a tree, a fire, a rock hole, or some similar centrally situated object. On a tjurunga, however, this plain symbol would normally have been replaced by a highly elaborated figure of ten, twenty, and even more concentric circles, or of a cleverly executed spiral containing the same number of convolutions. Similarly, single lines and half-circles are rarely to be found: they are generally doubled, trebled, or repeated even more often. Apart from being expressed in this careful elaboration of the simple constituent figures, the skill of the native artist found an outlet in a careful arrangement of these individual symbols into a pleasing and balanced pattern. Unity of design was evident in most of the innumerable groupings of symbols effected by the Aranda artists on their ceremonial objects. The best of them also showed a keen feeling for the beauty of line and contour; and some of the Aranda series of free-hand concentric circles are remarkable not merely for their elaboration but also for their sheer beauty. The sound judgment of the artists in combining colours tastefully is perhaps best evidenced in the patterns that once adorned the persons of their ceremonial actors; and it is a pity that so little attempt has been made to save these

[3

from oblivion. Limited though they were by the severe medium they had chosen, the Aranda artists had developed considerable skill in mastering basic problems of composition, drawing, and colour; and their best work was notable for its fine feeling for balance and for rhythm.

The initiated Aranda men were always deeply moved by their sacred art; and there have also been numerous Europeans, often incapable of fully appreciating the symbolism underlying the patterns, who have nevertheless been stirred to a sincere appreciation of their balance, rhythm, and intrinsic beauty. White Australians have occasionally used these symbols themselves and obtained some striking effects. One of the finest university halls in Australia is that of the University of Western Australia, whose ceiling with its artistic designs embodying richly coloured native symbols has aroused great admiration among most of the visitors who have been privileged to see it. A form of representational art which deals not with living, moving creatures and human beings, but rather with the patterns left behind by them, is not necessarily devoid of deep emotional appeal. I have recently found confirmation for my view in the remarks of an English art critic* who writes on the designs of ancient Celtic art as follows:

> Suppose an artist wanted to reproduce the emotional effect of a ritual dance in which the dancers trace a pattern on the ground. The modern traveller would photograph the dancers as they stand at a given moment. A conventional modern artist, with a mind debauched by naturalism, would draw them in the same kind of way. This would be a silly thing to do, because the emotional effect of the dance depends not on any instantaneous posture but on the traced pattern. The sensible thing would be to leave out the dancers altogether, and draw the pattern by itself. This certainly is the explanation of much "primitive" art which at first sight appears altogether non-representative: spirals, mazes, plaits and so forth. I think that, for example, it may possibly be the explanation of the strange curvilinear designs which are so characteristic of pre-Christian Celtic art in the La Tène period. These patterns produce a powerful and very peculiar emotional effect, which I can best describe as a mixture of voluptuousness and terror. This effect is certainly not accidental. The Celtic artists knew what they were doing; and I imagine that they produced this emotional reaction for religious or magical reasons. I conjecture that the state of mind may originally have been evoked by the dance-patterns of their religious ceremonies, and that the patterns we possess may be representations of this.

From this brief survey of traditional Aranda art two facts emerge which will explain the great and spontaneous enthusiasm for Western techniques of painting that has become manifest among the Aranda artists during the past decade or so. Firstly, it must be admitted that the old style of pictorial art had reached its highest stage of development centuries before the advent of the whites to Australia. Its patterns had become traditional, and few new combinations were possible to the younger artists. White artists, ignorant of the symbolism underlying the original

* R. G. Collingwood, *The Principles of Art*, 1937, p. 55.

4]

figures, could well achieve new designs based on them where the native painter would be inhibited from attempting fresh patterns by the weight of accumulated tradition. Such expanded designs as those on the ceiling of the Perth University Hall no longer attempt to relate a tale or to describe a scene; they are purely recombinations of aboriginal symbols intended to produce the maximum elaboration of an artistic design without any regard for the telling of a coherent story. It is a truism that any style of art which has reached its highest stage of development is doomed to decline. Once the great masters have expressed all that is possible in a certain form of one medium, artists of succeeding generations will wisely attempt to explore new avenues. Had foreign artistic ideas kept on coming into Australia before the arrival of the whites, the younger Aranda men would inevitably have allowed themselves to be influenced by them. The art form remained supreme partly because of its intimate association with religious ideas which, as is well-known, are strongly conservative, and partly because of the isolation of Australia from the art centres of other countries. That it would be a great loss to ourselves if the traditional art of the aborigines were to vanish completely, I should be the first to admit. But before it can survive, its figures and patterns will have to be adapted for use on new European articles introduced into the native environment. One of the best suggestions is that made by Dr L. Adam, of the Melbourne University, who has suggested that the natives should be given instruction in carpet weaving in the Persian style so that they could "manufacture valuable rugs showing aboriginal designs and aboriginal colours".

This is a splendid suggestion, which I should like to see being carried out in the near future. It will not, however, obviate the second grave defect of traditional Aranda art—its inability to achieve its full effect independent of verbal explanations. An artist who is working in an art form that can never encompass its emotional appeal without outside help will turn with a sense of relief and a glow of enthusiasm to another art form, using the same medium, that will enable him to express himself directly and unaided to his audience. In the old pictorial art form the limited number of symbols available had always acted as a severe barrier to a full understanding of the completed design. As stated earlier, a circle could be interpreted in many ways; and as long as the artist continued to think of his finished design as a sort of glorified map or diagram, no real improvement in representational pictorial art was possible. Native songs show how fine were the Australian artistic gifts as regards sense of rhythm, delight in exact shades of meaning, and a sense of the dominant mood of a landscape. In these songs a wonderfully developed poetic diction offered the native poets an opportunity for releasing their pent-up creative energies. In the realm of pictorial art the traditional habit of looking at everything from above limited the vision of the artist and frustrated his endeavours to express himself with freedom and clarity.

The day of liberation came when white men first showed coloured pictures to the natives. Probably few of these were of any great artistic value. But the natives now

[5

gazed with delight upon a world depicted as seen by eyes that have stopped staring at the ground in search of tracks and are looking instead at the landscape itself—a landscape filled with animals and human figures that need no further explanation or interpretation.

One disadvantage of these first European pictures in native eyes was the fact that they did not reflect the Central Australian environment; their emotional appeal was seriously lessened by the fact that they depicted scenes and human beings that were un-Australian and un-native. A new era for the Aranda artists began when several white Australian painters, notably Arthur Murch, Rex Battarbee, John Gardner, and William Rowell, arrived in Central Australia, where they began translating familiar landscapes and familiar native figures on to paper and canvas. The Aranda folk watched them intently and with evident fascination. At last they were viewing a new pictorial art which was capable of setting the trees, rocks, animals, and persons of their own environment as vividly before the eyes of admiring spectators as their own rich verse had once conjured them up on the songs whose cadences had delighted the ears of Aranda audiences.

Rex Battarbee himself has told the remainder of the story in this book. It is a story which has just begun; and I feel that it is only fair to ask art critics who detect some obvious failings and occasional clumsinesses in the use of a new medium in the illustrations of this book to remember that they are witnessing in these pictures only the first surgings of a liberated artistic impulse. In 1935 it would have been easy to prove that no full-blooded Australian aboriginal would ever be capable of mastering European techniques of painting; today one of the chief complaints levelled against Albert Namatjira is the charge that he is purely a "copyist" in that he paints exactly like a European artist! This is an interesting change in many ways; it also contains, however, a grudging admission that a member of a race which had been regarded without scientific grounds for over one hundred and fifty years as genetically incapable of learning European techniques had unexpectedly acquired mastery of one of these techniques to such an amazing degree that his work had become virtually indistinguishable from that of a white artist. Albert Namatjira, in short, is one of those gifted aborigines who has destroyed the myth of the constitutional incapacity of the Australian native to learn and to apply methods learnt from Europeans. For that reason alone Albert Namatjira will always deserve from us unstinted honour and recognition. In his best paintings he has put on record the beauty and the colour of Central Australia with a warmth that proclaims his deep love for his homeland. The numerous deviations that have been achieved from Albert Namatjira's style of painting by the younger Hermannsburg artists prove that painting in the Western tradition has come to stay in Central Australia: it is now clearly affording an important outlet for the artistic drives of the natives themselves. Water-colour painting at Hermannsburg is being enriched by the experiences of the artists: in the best works of Otto Pareroultja, for instance, I seem to find expressed through a pictorial medium the same kind of distinctive Aranda feeling for balance, love of repetition and design, and sure sense of rhythm, that give such glorious vitality to their best verse.

A final word of praise is due to the writer of this book, Mr Rex Battarbee, whose stimulating influence and guidance have assisted all of our first aboriginal painters while they were striving to gain technical mastery over their medium. He has always helped his dark artist friends with unwearying readiness without attempting to curb their own inclinations. It is mainly through his efforts that the impulse towards pictorial expression possessed by our natives has been directed into channels that have already produced work memorable in the field of Australian Art.

T. G. H. STREHLOW

[7

I

INTRODUCTION

★

ON SEVERAL painting trips to Inland Australia I used to find the aborigines very interested in my work as a water-colour artist and I usually carried drawing books and coloured crayons for their use. The natives, both young and old, never tired of watching me at work and, although they are a shy people, I could usually get them to draw for me. The children especially loved making drawings. Their skill in drawing moving objects from memory always impressed me and this ability no doubt sprang from their wonderful powers of observation.

On the first caravan trip in 1932 to Central Australia, my artist friend, John A. Gardner, and I made contacts with hundreds of aborigines and out of these contacts have grown lasting friendships. It was not until our second caravan trip to Central Australia in 1934 that we met the now-famous aboriginal water-colour artist, Albert Namatjira. On our first trip Albert was away from Hermannsburg at Henburg cattle station building a stockyard. Being a good craftsman, ambitious and industrious, he was prepared to go to a neighbouring station to make a few shillings with which to satisfy his longing for something more than the ordinary station rations and bush tucker. Because of this desire Albert Namatjira's entry into the world of art was probably delayed two years. If he had been at Hermannsburg in 1932 and seen our paintings of his country, his desire to paint would unquestionably have been awakened. Fate takes her own time and the reason may have been that Albert was to have only one contact so as to have the least outside interference possible. I am sure these primitive people work better under one master; and they never forget their first approach to learning anything, whereby they set their standard. Even in 1934 Albert Namatjira never received any assistance from either Gardner or myself, our first meeting occurring only when we were about to leave Hermannsburg. After spending some months painting in the district we had a collection of pictures which Pastor F. W. Albrecht, Superintendent of the Finke River mission at Hermannsburg, saw and wanted us to exhibit at the mission so that the mission natives as well as the whites might enjoy them. It has always been Pastor Albrecht's belief that the aborigines

[9

should have equal opportunity with the white members of the mission staff to appreciate life. I feel sure he did not realize at the time that his action was to set a spark to one of the greatest art movements in history.

Pastor Albrecht, a progressive, was at that time racking his brain to think of some means of employing his large native population so as to give them something more than the meagre supplies that a struggling mission or a government ration could provide. In his wildest dreams he would never have thought it possible that, within thirteen years, one year's sales of paintings by these men would have totalled £3000.

The exhibition at Hermannsburg in 1934 gave the two white artists a great deal of satisfaction, since they felt that no white audience would ever have shown such enthusiasm. The artists took it as a compliment to the faithfulness with which they portrayed the country which the natives knew so well. For two days the exhibition continued and attendances never waned; a large number of the three hundred aborigines sat entranced by the pictures for hours at a time. Little did I realize that in this group of people was a man who viewed the pictures very differently from the average person and that that man—Albert Namatjira—was destined to become a fine artist. He has since become the best known Australian aboriginal of any generation, who, through his art, has given the remnants of his race a new hope in their future by creating an impression that they have a place alongside the white people who brought a new civilization to their land.

The same white people have made it difficult for the black man who has been isolated in his Stone Age for so many centuries. The white man came from countries where the economic struggle for life and existence made him keen, made him a good pioneer who would develop a new country. The Australian aboriginal had been isolated for so long that he had built up a narrow tribal code which could not withstand the onrush of a more virile civilization. The white settler did not intend harm, but the clash was too sudden for stone-age man, unable to adjust himself to the new conditions. Unfortunately most of our governments, aided by anthropologists, have followed the defeatist plan of segregation. I feel that the only successful plan for the aboriginal's future is to allow him time to adjust himself to the new conditions, with a view to taking his place eventually alongside the white man in society.

The story of the rise of Albert Namatjira is like fiction. After seeing the exhibition of paintings of his own country at Hermannsburg, he realized its beauty and colour for the first time. Up to this Albert had only seen coloured pictures in books, mostly Biblical pictures in the mission school and church. These pictures did not leave a great impression on a man who had not travelled beyond his own tribal area. It was different when he saw faithful paintings of his own country which he knew perfectly. There can be no doubt that to Albert, after studying the pictures for hours, colour was the most important thing about them. He has never shown any desire to portray his country in black and white.

10]

There is no denying that Albert was a born artist, but he was also ambitious and had a wife and a large family to keep. The fact that the two white artists had travelled from Melbourne in a motor caravan and had made two such trips to his country made a deep impression on Albert's mind. In art he saw a way out of his poor existence of slender rations and no money. Some years afterwards, when Albert had a ready sale for his pictures at high prices, he said to me that, before he started painting, no matter how hard he worked—whether at carpentry, blacksmithing, building stockyards, or working with Afghans as a camel-boy on the train between Oodnadatta and Alice Springs before the railway was put through—he could get rations and clothes but never even a sixpence. "Things are different now!" he exclaimed.

John Gardner and I left Hermannsburg for Melbourne soon after that exhibition in 1934. Just before we left Pastor Albrecht came to me and said that Albert had approached him. He wanted to paint in water-colours. Would we buy him some paints, paper, and brushes? Pastor Albrecht was prepared to help the man in case he had any latent talent and asked me for a list of materials to buy. This I gave him and also offered to help by giving Albert a few points in painting. If work was posted on to me, I would try to correct it. Pastor Albrecht gave a very wide answer. "You will be back again and then you can take Albert with you on a painting trip."

In 1936 I returned alone to Hermannsburg without the caravan—since I intended getting a team of camels at the mission—and with the hope that Albert, the native who wanted to paint, would still be interested. I can tell you I was moved when I reached the mission. The first native to speak to me was Albert, who poured out his soul, saying that he had been waiting for nearly two years, sometimes lying awake at night thinking of the time I would return and take him out on a painting expedition as a camel-boy, living in hope that I would teach him to paint in water-colours for his services. Albert showed me a few crude water-colours which he had painted without lessons; but he was not satisfied and had given up the idea until I returned. He went on to tell me of the wonderful places he would take me to.

I thought a native would find water-colours a very difficult medium, since I had had to work hard for years to be able to express myself freely in paint. I have often wondered why I was the person picked by Fate for this job: my sole assets were that I was country-bred and a lover of the bush, that I was practically self-taught, at least in water-colour painting, and that I had developed a style of water-colour painting which was my own. This last point worried me for a while when I had to decide on a method of teaching Albert. I felt I had to be honest, so I taught Albert my own style. This clicked and no doubt was the most important point of our contact. I felt that colour was my strongest point and in my method I was able to take Albert right back to Nature. I was very nervous about the word "colour". Albert's knowledge of English was limited. His main language was Arunta and strangely enough the most freely used word in that language is the word "colour", which occurs in almost every sentence.

[11

It has several meanings according to the way it is used, but usually means "finish", and in some cases "ready to start".

I set Albert off with coloured crayons and cardboard; but he was not satisfied with that. He wanted to paint in the same medium as I was doing—no half measures with this man. My greatest surprise came after we had been out for two weeks and were painting in Palm Valley. Albert brought along a painting of the Amphitheatre to which I had not even seen him put a brush. I immediately saw his talent. Here was a man, a full-blooded member of a race considered the lowest type in the world, who had in two weeks absorbed my colour sense. I felt that he had done the job so well that he had no need to learn more from me about colour. At the time I well remember writing home to my people saying that this man would become famous as an artist. From then on I simply corrected any faults that occurred in such things as composition. He brought in only one picture with a fatal mistake in composition. It was a blessing he had to be corrected only once. He had an unspoilt mind and had nothing to unlearn.

Albert was with me for two months at this time. The first month was spent in the Finke River Valley and Palm Valley, James Range, and the second month in the Macdonnell Range at Redbank Gorge and Arumber Gorge, Gosse's Range, and Gilbert Springs. Albert was marvellous as a camel-boy and spoilt me for other natives because he was thoroughly reliable and always keen to do his job. In this case he was especially keen, since he wanted to learn something from me and had ambition and intelligence. If anything went wrong with the saddles or camels he could fix it.

This was the only period during which Albert had any tuition in water-colours. I have been out with him on later painting trips but I have never given him lessons because I felt that he already knew enough and I wanted him to show something of his own outlook and personality in his work. I have always believed that no ordinary white man could have done what Albert did in such a short time. He had such a grasp of water-colours and was such a good draughtsman that he could go on improving under his own steam. He certainly can correct his own work and has no difficulty in choosing a subject. He also has a wonderful natural sense of balance in his pictures.

The leading South Australian artist, Hans Heysen, bought some of Albert's early work, including a painting of a gum-tree. I asked Heysen if it would be wise for Albert to go down to Adelaide to improve his knowledge of art. "Definitely not," was the reply. "Why, Albert knows too much already!"

Albert Namatjira painting at Standly Chasm, Macdonnell Range,
Central Australia in 1946 when Their Royal Highnesses the Duke
and Duchess of Gloucester made a special trip from Alice Springs
to see Albert at work.

Exhibition of water-colours by Otto Pareroultja at the Hermannsburg Mission before the pictures went to Otto's first exhibition in
1947 at Melbourne.

II

ALBERT NAMATJIRA

*

ALBERT NAMATJIRA, a pure-blooded aboriginal of the Aranda or Arunta tribe, Central Australia, was born at Hermannsburg on 28th July 1902. His family name means "flying white-ant". His mother, Emilie, was the wife of Jonathan Namatjira. Albert's mother died during the big drought which ended in 1929; but although she did not see her son reach fame, his father is still alive and takes pride in his artist son. He has often thanked me for what I did for Albert, and he never tires of telling strangers that *he* is Albert's father.

While still in his teens, Albert married Rubena, a tall pure-blooded daughter of one of the leaders of a Loritja group living on the edge of western Arunta country, and has since reared a healthy family of five sons and three daughters. His is one of the finest examples of an Australian aboriginal family one could wish to meet. It gives the lie to the notion that the Australian aborigines are a dying race. How is it possible, you ask, for such a family as this to flourish today? Without the Finke River mission, which was opened in 1877 by Lutheran missionaries at Hermannsburg and which continues its activities today under a different group of the same Church, it would not have been possible. The mission station at present consists fortunately of nearly a million acres of Arunta tribal country, bounded on the north by the Macdonnell Ranges and on the south by the James Range, with the Finke River cutting right across. There is a wonderful variety of country both as a hunting ground and as a suitable country for the artist, with its beautiful mountain ranges and river valleys, its magnificent trees and red sandhills. Over three generations these people have had time to adjust themselves to a changing civilization. Their nearest town, Alice Springs, is eighty miles away. They may visit it at times but are not encouraged to stay too long; otherwise they might be swallowed up in one of those blackfellows' graveyards, the slum areas of Australian towns and cities.

The policy of the mission at Hermannsburg, apart from the religious training, is that rations are given exclusively to people who are willing to work, excepting the aged, the infirm, and children. Some are trained to do different classes of work. Many are employed as stockmen, the mission being almost self-supporting as a cattle run. Others work in a tannery. Here men are paid in cash for supplying skins, while others are tanners who treat the skins, or leather workers and bootmakers. Some women also help with bootmaking and others do fancywork. Other workers are employed in the gardens and on odd jobs about the mission.

One of the happiest accidents is that the mission has become the main home of the Arunta tribe. With them there has developed a family life of which they are proud. They do not suffer from the inferiority complex that stultifies these aborigines who frequent towns and stations.

Albert himself is a big man judged by any standards. He would be an outstanding man no matter what race he belonged to, and he has all the qualities of eminence. He has often told me he must be doing something. If he sits down for more than a day at a time, he finds life irksome. He is very ambitious, especially for a pure-blooded aboriginal, has a lot of reasoning power, and will not take a mere "Yes" or "No" for an answer. If a case is clearly stated to him, he can and will accept the light. Albert is also of commanding appearance with a quiet dignity characteristic of his race. As he has become more famous, this quality has become even more noticeable. During the last few years he has put on too much weight and a couple of years ago was over eighteen stone—far too much for anyone of Albert's height, let alone an aboriginal whose ancestors for generations have always been lean. The cause of this increase in weight has been the change from the bush life of a nomad who had to be always on the move to get enough food to live, and whose food was mostly proteins and coarse vegetables and fruits and whole seeds. When the aboriginal gets the taste of white man's food, he thinks it wonderful, and easy to prepare, but he does not realize how important it is to have a balanced diet. In their natural state, during good seasons, the aborigines have a balanced diet; but usually, when they are living on white man's food, their diet is mostly of meat and white flour. They make damper of the flour and if they are not working on a cattle station, damper is their staple food.

The white man is partly to blame for this, because he has not educated the native as to the value of a proper diet. There is no doubt that white flour has been one of the main causes of aboriginal disease. The aboriginal is not used to a starchy diet.

Albert's case is a very interesting example. Being a man of means, he naturally went in exclusively for white man's food: damper was the standby, with tea, sugar, jams, and tinned goods as extras. On top of this he bought a motor truck. That meant he did not do as much walking as formerly, and his weight increased so much that it began to tell on his health. Two years ago Dr J. de Vidas of Alice Springs diagnosed his case as a severe form of heart trouble and Albert seemed for several months to be failing in health. His poor health affected the quality of his painting. Early in 1948 the doctor went to Queensland but before leaving Alice Springs he had a long talk with Albert about his diet, telling him to eat plenty of meat, vegetables, fruit, and bush tucker and to eschew damper and sweets. Later in the year, at Hermannsburg, I met Albert soon after he had returned from a three months' painting trip through country in the western James Range, where he and his wife Rubena had travelled on camels. Albert was looking very well and had regained much of his former bloom. I mentioned this to him and he said he felt like a new man and that, thanks to the Alice Springs doctor, he had cut out damper and sugar. He laughingly said that Rubena ate most of the sugar they had and, as she was of the lean type, it did not do her any damage. They had had plenty of meat and bush tucker and the only sweets he'd eaten were some honey ants, which Rubena was expert at collecting. He said he always felt well when he had plenty of honey ants in his diet. "See that mountain range over there," he pointed out, "I can walk to the top of that without difficulty now. Not so a year ago." His work regained its former sparkle. This helps to show the character of the man whose rise to fame is like a fairy tale.

The romantic story of Albert Namatjira could not have been planned by man alone. How should it come about that Albert was the first of his race to prove himself in the art world in the white man's medium of water-colours and to make people of all nations look with renewed interest at his race? If he had not been a success, it would have been odds on against another aboriginal of his tribe having the courage and energy to succeed in this field of art, for aborigines are discouraged by failures in new ventures. But Albert never looked back, and the more successful he was, the harder he worked.

This itself is amazing to one who has had anything to do with Australian aborigines. Generally speaking the average native is lazy and, when he has a few shillings or some food, wants to sit down until it is finished. Not so with Namatjira. Success only spurred him on. He always tried to improve his work, even in face of the greatest temptation to any artist—being able to sell all his pictures. Albert had even more than this to conquer, something that the average white man is not up against to the same extent. Compared with his hundreds of poor relations and tribal connections, he had untold wealth, which the law of the aboriginies demanded be shared. They knew no other law, since they had lived a communal life for centuries, all food and belongings being shared among their tribal relations. Albert had been through all this and with all his wealth he did not flinch from his tribal duty. Of course he knew no other law, but who else would have continued to work even harder when in one year at least £1200 of his income went on food for his relatives and their relatives. At times he observed to me that some of his people were always asking for food or money, but this did not stop him from painting more and more pictures, which would be sold for the same purpose. This has gone on for twelve years without a break. Along with his great qualities of character Albert is an artist from the depths of his heart, since no one would work so hard under these conditions unless he loved his work.

His greatest critics have been anthropologists and artists who have a different outlook on art. Their main argument was that he should be painting his own aboriginal art on bark shields, and so on. If they understood more of Arunta tribal law, they would soon realize that there is very little art that a man of Albert's age and group could practise without breaking that law. In the Arunta tribe, as in most of the Central Australian tribes, men are permitted to draw only concentric circles and wavy lines, such as animal tracks. They are not even allowed to draw animals, which is the kind of drawing the aborigines nearer the coast, such as the Arnhem Land natives, are expected to do. Most of their tribal drawings are symbolical, and are drawn by the older men on their most sacred churungas and bull-roarers. These drawings have different meanings, known only by the owners of these sacred objects. The concentric circles on these may mean any totem such as a kangaroo, emu, or snake according to the owner's totem.

The Australian aboriginal did not have the complete range of colours. He was restricted to four: red, yellow, white, and black. Not having blue made it impossible for him to paint realistic landscapes. I have not seen any painted shields or bark paintings by primitive Arunta tribesmen, so to a man of Albert's realistic tastes and ambitions there was nothing in his own art that could possibly have satisfied his personal wants. But when he saw that exhibition of paintings of his own country at Hermannsburg in 1934, it was a new field opened up to him and one which would not offend tribal law.

I am sure that when Albert started to paint he had no idea what fame and fortune were in the offing. Looking back now over the past twelve years, it would be a poor soul who would deny him his present honour and glory; whereas Albert was a very proud man when he sold his first water-colour in 1936 for five shillings.

Mr W. H. Gill of the Fine Arts Society's Gallery, Melbourne, was the first person to give Albert Namatjira his big chance to prove his worth as an artist to the world, when he offered the use of his Gallery and services free of cost. This exhibition, held in November 1938, was opened by Lady Huntingfield, the wife of the Governor of Victoria at that time. Lady Huntingfield was interested because she had met Albert when on a visit to Central Australia. This exhibition of forty-one water-colours, priced at one to six guineas each, all sold within a few days.

Towards the end of 1939 his next exhibition was held at the South Australian Society of Arts Gallery, Adelaide, when the whole collection of forty-one water-colours were sold at prices from two to eight guineas each. At this exhibition the National Gallery of South Australia bought the now well-known water-colour, "Haast Bluff (Alumbaura)". This picture, although a fairly early Namatjira, has held its own in the Australian water-colour section in the Adelaide Art Gallery even when placed alongside paintings by our most famous artists.

From 1939 to 1944 Albert held no exhibition of his work, mainly because of the demand for his pictures in Alice Springs during the war years, when a big military

16]

camp was stationed there in control of the transport to supply Darwin. Strangely, the Alice Springs people were not interested in Albert's pictures until the Army personnel showed their appreciation.

Albert's third exhibition was held in Melbourne during April 1944, when he sold over £800 worth of pictures at prices ranging from ten to thirty-five guineas each. In 1944 the Melbourne Bread and Cheese Club published *The Art of Albert Namatjira*, by C. P. Mountford, with a foreword by R. H. Croll. This book, now in its fourth edition, has ten of his paintings reproduced in natural colours.

The next exhibition was held in Sydney in 1945 at Anthony Hordern's Art Gallery under the management of Mr A. K. Marsden. This exhibition was run free of cost to the artist. It was a startling success, the whole collection of forty-four pictures selling for the sum of £1000. All but one of the pictures had been sold twenty minutes after Professor A. P. Elkin opened the exhibition.

The year 1946 saw two exhibitions by the artist. At the first, early in the year at Adelaide, all his forty-four water-colours were sold for more than £1000 at prices of up to forty guineas each. At the second in Perth towards the end of the year, thirty-three pictures were sold at prices ranging from eighteen to fifty guineas each.

That year was an important one for the artist, as the Films Division of the Commonwealth Department of Information with C. P. Mountford, director, Lee Robinson, co-director, and Axel Poignant, photographer, worked for several months in Central Australia on a documentary film in 16-millimetre Kodachrome on the art and life of Albert Namatjira. This film was shown in commercial picture theatres throughout Australia in 1948 as *Namatjira the Painter*.

The year 1947 saw two more exhibitions by Albert Namatjira. He held his first in Alice Springs at Griffiths House, where he sold the whole collection of fourteen water-colours, at prices from eighteen to forty-five guineas each to the value of £416. This is the most remarkable exhibition the artist has ever held and probably, from a population basis, nothing like it has ever happened before. The Alice Springs population at the time was under two thousand; when it is compared with Melbourne or Sydney, an interesting fact emerges. The enthusiasm shown speaks volumes for the artistic susceptibilities of the people of Alice Springs, which most people of the large cities would regard as just another bush town of no importance.

This could not have happened ten years earlier; but the war gave Alice Springs people a new interest in the arts, mainly through the Alice Springs Arts Club which ran for some years during the war with the help of visiting artists, musicians, and writers. Here, in Albert Namatjira, was a prophet who *was* appreciated in his own country.

Later in the year Albert held a successful exhibition in Brisbane, thus completing a series of exhibitions in all the larger Australian capitals.

In November 1948 he reached his highest total sales when at his third Melbourne exhibition, a decade after his first, he sold forty-six water-colours for £1519 at prices ranging from eighteen to fifty-five guineas each.

This is an imposing list of exhibitions. The National Galleries of Adelaide, Perth, and Brisbane have bought Namatjira's pictures, while a great proportion of his work has gone overseas. Even people as far away as Iceland are interested in his work; no doubt some of his pictures of the Red Centre help to warm up the homes of the people there.

One of the most amazing things in this amazing story is that Albert Namatjira has gained world-wide fame without ever having seen an art gallery. Indeed, he has seen only two small towns—Alice Springs and Ooodnadatta. The only exhibition of his own work which he has attended, apart from one at Hermannsburg, was that at Alice Springs.

This aboriginal artist, who was thought to be a freak—"the only great aboriginal artist of modern times"—today takes a new place in history as the forerunner of one of the greatest movements we have seen in Australian Art. Mr A. K. Marsden, director of Anthony Hordern's Art Gallery, Sydney, who is recognized as one of the foremost authorities on art in Australia, says that this is the most important art development we have had in Australia for the past hundred years. And it comes *from the heart of the country*, from Albert Namatjira's own people of the Arunta.

For ten years Albert has been a man of means, because he is the best-seller among Australian artists. Wherever he has held an exhibition of his work, there has always been a frantic rush to buy his pictures. I am sure this would be the case if he exhibited in any of the important cities of the world. Because of this popularity an Advisory Council was formed at Hermannsburg in 1943 to help the artist in his affairs and to try and keep up the high standard of his work. The Council has been a great success; mainly because of it Albert has not become spoilt but has persisted in trying to improve his work instead of going in for the mass production, which would have been the natural reaction of an artist who could probably sell ten times the number of pictures he paints. This control also has given other men of his own tribe an opportunity to sell good work at lower prices. These men had their chance during the war, when there were thousands of soldiers stationed in Alice Springs.

First the natives started painting on boomerangs and wommeras, which had a ready sale while the war lasted. Through this experience they had practice in drawing and acquired technique in using water-colours. By the time the war was finished the demand for curios had ended; but several of these men had established themselves as water-colourists and have continued to make a good living from their art. Because of Albert's success, it was natural that he would have imitators among the men of his tribe. I have often come across a lone native sketching; he would sheepishly say that he was just trying to see what he could do. Many of these men never got past that first attempt, while others have told me that it was too difficult to be an artist. The tendency was to copy Albert and, since Albert is a very good craftsman, it was very difficult to make them see that his is not the only kind of art. The missionaries also took the view that, if Albert was such a great artist, his must be the true art, so that men whose work bore most resemblance to his were encouraged.

Because there had been so much criticism that Albert was only a copyist of my style, I was on the look-out for men who had the ability and the strength of character to be original. I felt that the natives were natural artists who needed only the chance and encouragement to express themselves.

The critics were hard on Albert. Being an artist, I could see what the natives were striving to say, so I felt it my duty to give any new men a chance to express themselves in their own way. I knew that Albert was a true artist and had to get a start from somebody, but I have never interfered with his work since he had his only tuition of two months in 1936. For him to be able to carry on alone since then and to be able to reach his present eminence as a water-colourist is proof that he knows how to express himself. Unquestionably his background as an aboriginal with a native training in childhood helped him. Men like Albert, who are living still in their own tribal country and amongst their own people, know the life history of every animal, tree, bird, or insect. Living in the open during all seasons, they have trained eyes and such keen powers of observation that learning to be an artist is child's play. This is where I think they have the advantage over the average city person who has lost most of these powers of observation because of his crowded life and the mass entertainment of radio, cinemas, and comic strips.

If an aboriginal was to make a name as an artist in the white man's medium, it was right that the first should be a man of Albert's ability. My first thought, when Albert started to paint, was to give him a chance to show that he was capable of proving that an Australian aboriginal was at least able to paint as well as a white artist. Albert has given the answer to this; but the main thing he lost in the process through his keenness to succeed was his aboriginal sense of decoration.

We in Australia have no purely Australian art or music. In the past we have naturally been influenced mostly by European art. Since the arrival of the first oversea artists, such as Conrad Martens, John Glover, and Louis Buvelot, our art has passed through all the different European movements, as it did when Tom Roberts returned from a visit to France with enthusiasm for the impressionist style of painting light and colour out of doors, a style so suitable for Australian conditions. All the different art movements have been outdated in Europe by the time they have become popular here.

Perhaps we can learn something from our aboriginal artists. At present there are several white artists trying to show us an Australian aboriginal form of art which is too forced to be of much value. The true primitive artist is too far removed from us to be of much assistance to present-day art. The Arunta artists are painting in our medium but are so isolated and have had so little assistance that they may be nearer a real Australian art than anyone has ever been in the past.

[19

III

EDWIN PAREROULTJA

★

THE FIRST remarkable event following Namatjira's adoption of European technique was a breakaway initiated by Edwin Pareroultja. Because Pareroultja was bold enough to express himself fully in paint, other men around him have felt that they too are free to express themselves according to their own temperament. The amazing thing is that so many men of the Arunta tribe have taken to water-colours naturally that one could be forgiven for thinking that they were the original water-colourists, not that the white man had brought the art to them. Anyone who has tried to paint in water-colours will know how difficult the medium is; but most of the aboriginal artists are soon able, with very little or no help, to paint well enough to use it as an expression of their own personality.

One of the reasons for this is that they are not burdened, like most students, with the "must" and "must not do", which really means that most art students are over-taught. No doubt the attitude the aborigines take is that if one of their own people like Albert Namatjira can paint successfully, why not they? When Edwin Pareroultja came along with more freedom and was accepted as an artist, the effect on the would-be artists was even stronger. Now they felt that they could paint in the way they wanted to do, unfettered by any rules. They believed they would be encouraged and that their work would be sold for them.

Albert Namatjira has proved himself a wonderful man and artist. Is it not even more remarkable to find in a small community of about three hundred people, ten artists who are able to make a living through the sale of their paintings? They are all keen on their work and would rather be painting pictures than doing anything else. The great advantage is that, because of Edwin's breakaway, they are all painting differently. A few men who originally followed Albert closely are now gradually breaking away from his style, mainly because of the success of Pareroultja and his brothers.

If an artist has originality plus something really worth saying, and can express himself, he will be able to make a place for himself. One wonders at times how many

The three Pareroultja brother artists at Hermannsburg.
From left to right, Edwin, Reuben and Otto.

Camel team returning from a painting trip crossing the flooded
Finke River. Otto Pareroultja is leading the camels.

more artists will arise from this group. Will they be able to hold their place, to make a living, or just to paint for the sheer love of it? There are others in this group who paint spasmodically, like Gustav Malbanka. Gustav did quite a lot of painting while he was in the Army at Alice Springs during the war years, but now he paints only occasionally, since he is one of the aboriginal pastoralists who have their herds of cattle on the aboriginal reserve.

The ten aboriginal artists featured in this book are at present making their living out of art. He would be a brave—or foolish—man who would say that this art movement was in full bloom. It may be only in its spring, with full summer to come. Time will tell. The development has been sudden; but from the vitality of the work shown by some of the lesser known men during the past year, I get the impression that it is going to reach even greater heights. At times the superintendent of the Hermannsburg mission has been worried over the size of the art growth; firstly, because a number of his best workers have taken up art as an occupation and secondly, because of the large incomes some of them make from the sale of their pictures. Naturally he is pleased they can make good money; but he knows that the mission cannot pay the ordinary workers on the mission the sums that most of the artists earn. Because of this he feels that the non-artist may become discontented, and the mission suffer.

Edwin Pareroultja, a pure-blooded aboriginal, was born at Hermannsburg on 23rd October 1918. He is the youngest of the tree Pareroultja artist brothers, the other two being Otto and Reuben. His family name means "the debris under a gum-tree". Edwin is married to Muriel, a daughter of Abel and Rosa, and they have three small daughters. Before he took up art, he was employed at odd jobs on the mission.

For at least ten years Edwin has been the outstanding athlete, white or black, at Hermannsburg and, probably, in Central Australia. Even when there were thousands of soldiers stationed in Alice Springs he was outstanding. He excels in running and jumping, and he would have made a champion footballer if he had had a chance, since he had all the gifts for it, and was 5 feet 7½ inches in height and 11 stone in weight. Dr Charles Duguid, that great lover of our aborigines, examined Edwin once and said he had never seen anyone with such good muscle development. Edwin has amazing dash and is a quick thinker. He is remarkably agile; when he was playing football at the mission, he seemed like a rubber ball and was in the air most of the time.

Edwin showed his quality as a runner when he made his first appearance in open company at a Red Cross sports meeting in Alice Springs, held on Foundation Day, 1944. He won both the 130-yards and the 75-yards races. Although the champions from the Army and the Allied Works Council were running, Edwin, a novice, was the only one on scratch, and ran barefooted.

In 1946 Edwin was taken to Victoria with Eli Rubuntja, another member of his tribe, to compete in the famous Stawell Gift, and also the Bendigo Easter Fair Gift. They were the guests of Mr and Mrs J. K. Moreton, Lake Bolac, for six weeks. Edwin did not strike form, and injured a leg muscle a week before the Stawell Gift. He ran in his heat, but broke down. Four days later at Bendigo he won a couple of heats, and then his leg gave more trouble.

His mate, Eli Rubuntja, the second string, who was very unfavourably handicapped, made a great impression. Although he was making his first appearance in public, he ran second in the final of the 100 yards at Stawell. Rubuntja ran six times at this Stawell meeting for three firsts and three seconds—a remarkable performance for a novice from the bush. The crowd gave him a marvellous ovation when he won heats and a semi-final. He ran even better at Bendigo, where he won a place in the final of the Easter Gift and the 75 yards. These two runners should have had a chance to prove their worth the following year in Victoria, but received no encouragement from the authorities who control them.

Edwin keeps his form surprisingly well, and can still more than hold his own in most events when the mission conducts its sports on Boxing Day, and Kaporilja Day, which is held on 1st October, the anniversary of the opening of the pipe-line that carries water from Kaporilja Springs four and a half miles away to the mission. On 1st October 1935 this water first flowed to the mission. The Misses Violet and Una Teatue, of Victoria, were the prime movers of this scheme, which indirectly has contributed to the art development that followed its completion.

In a novelty race I have seen Edwin clear a post-and-rail stockyard, 5 feet 3 inches high, built on a rising sandhill, when he jumped into and out of the yard. All the other runners vaulted over these fences. I have also seen him in novelty races jump bare-footed on to a motor-truck with sides 5 feet high, placing one foot on the side, which was one inch wide, the other in the floor of the truck, and then over. He would not seem to be the type one might expect to turn to art for an occupation, although artists are not turned out in a mould.

The greatest impression any artist has ever made on me was on 25th October 1943, when Edwin showed me his first water-colour. He had a painting on each side of the paper; both were of Mount Sonder, a landmark near Hermannsburg. One of these, though incomplete, showed the influence of Albert Namatjira but the other, which showed a complete breakaway from Namatjira, is reproduced in this book (Plate V). The picture was painted in the three primary colours, yellow, red, and blue. I noticed that Edwin was at the time wearing a yellow shirt of the same shade as the yellow in the picture. The drawing, sense of decoration, colour, and power were amazing for a first attempt. This painting made me feel very humble. Here was the type of native artist I was looking for. He seemed to be ready-made, so from that day I advised him not to copy Albert Namatjira's work or my own, since we were the only artists he knew at the time. I have jealously tried to guard him from outside influences.

I told him if he was in trouble with his art to come and ask for help, but I dared not interfere with one who had so much natural ability. Only after two years did I once spend about an hour showing Edwin how he could keep his washes cleaner. That was all the tuition he had. I have often had talks with him, recommending him to put down on paper what he sees himself and not to be influenced by other people, even if they are critical of his work, telling him that his best art is his own. Edwin has kept to his own style, which shows the character of the man.

My opinion is that unless an artist is of strong character and sticks to his own ideas, his work will not last. So many very clever artists keep changing their styles, emulating those of the most successful men around them, thereby denying their own a chance to mature.

Edwin, I feel, is a genius, because at his best he does amazing work. It is so simple and at times appears to be carelessly done. But when one comes to analyse it, it is sound and offends no canons of art. It is unconscious. It *is* the work of a genius. Compared with Albert Namatjira, whose paintings are more photographic, Edwin has a sense of aboriginal decoration that Albert's work lacks. This sense of decoration stands apart from composition or design, and is the outstanding quality in our Australian aborigines' art. The Arunta, more than most tribes, had to depend on this sense of decoration, because all its tribal drawings were symbolic. Of this group of artists Edwin Pareroultja has the greatest sense of decoration. He is also a natural colourist, using an amazing variety of colour combinations in different strengths that always seem to harmonize. He is also outstanding among the Arunta group in that he uses colour for the sheer joy of using it. At the same time he maintains a luminous quality that is typical of the colour of the country and the artistic licence he sometimes allows himself in forcing his colour helps to give this effect. Edwin also has a colour pattern which is his own and yet is another aboriginal quality. He keeps his colour planes apart, but they work into a pattern through his sense of decoration. This breaking up of his planes makes his work appear less photographic, but he is still able to maintain perspective. His pictures are also full of light.

Edwin's drawing is sounder, simpler, and stronger than that of most of the other aboriginal artists, and this gives his work a feeling of strength (Plate VIII). His paintings are also full of feeling because he is very emotional, and, being a rapid worker and thinker, he is able to express these moods in his pictures. As a result, his work contains more variety than that of any of his fellow artists.

The outstanding feature of this artist is that he is *himself*; a being full of colour, strength, and emotional feeling, and so his work is vital. It gives one a shock at first sight, because it is new, but if one is prepared to spend time studying it, one will soon be drawn to it. There is no doubt Pareroultja is a very great artist and there is no knowing how far he will go or what heights he will reach. His work is like that of Gauguin, the French post-impressionist, yet he has never heard of Gauguin or his work.

The Melbourne National Gallery bought two of Edwin Pareroultja's water-colours in 1946, and the Sydney National Gallery bought his "Amulda Gorge" in 1947. He held his first exhibition of water-colours at the Athenaeum Art Gallery, Melbourne, in November 1946, when the whole collection of fifty pictures was sold in three days. H.R.H. the Duchess of Gloucester was very interested in Edwin's work when she saw it on a trip to Central Australia in 1946, and asked to have a preview of his Melbourne exhibition.

In November 1947 Edwin held his second exhibition at Anthony Hordern's Art Gallery, Sydney, when all the pictures in his collection of forty-eight water-colours were sold. His next exhibition was held in 1948 at the Claude Hotchin Galleries, Perth.

Edwin's work is not as popular with the general public as that of Albert Namatjira—Albert's is easier to understand! It is the thinking type of person who is interested in Edwin's work, and most artists and critics prefer it. Edwin is a good contrast to Albert Namatjira and the right man to follow him. It is interesting to note that the Melbourne and Sydney National Art Galleries, which have none of Albert's water-colours, have bought Edwin's. Up to the present Edwin has not shown such enthusiasm for his work as Albert has, and he does not get out on such long painting trips. If ever he does, he will give us more surprises.

Albert has to work harder because he is slower, more painstaking, and more ambitious; but a big factor is that Albert was older when he started to paint and had a harder life behind him. Aborigines have a long youth and do not seem to settle down till they are about twenty-four years of age—some much older than that. Another reason why Edwin does not go on such long trips is that he has a young family. Arunta people are very fond of their children, and Edwin does not like being away from home for too long at a time. The younger men are also more afraid of the bush natives, who might get hold of them and put them through some tribal ceremony.

Another problem the artists have when they go on a painting trip is to get suitable men to go with them. First of all they need someone to look after their horses or camels and to keep them company. Artists become interested in their work while painting and may want to stay days or even weeks in one camping place; but the men who are not painting get very tired of one place if there are only a few in the party. I remember camping with Albert at Glen Helen Gorge ten years ago; we had been painting in the one place for three weeks and five days when I decided to move on. I said to Albert that we would change our camp, and also remarked that I still could find more work to do at that spot. Albert surprised me by saying that he would not mind staying there as long as that again whereas, before he took on painting, a day or two in one place was enough. "It's hard," he said, "to get anybody to stay with me in these camps."

During the winter of 1948 Edwin decided to go on a painting trip to Ayers Rock, which is about two hundred miles south-west from Hermannsburg. This was Edwin's

24]

Otto Pareroultja painting along the edge of the Finke River
while his son Trevor takes a keen interest.

Flood waters encroach on the artists' camp at the Finke Gorge,
Glen Helen, Macdonnell Range. Otto Pareroultja and his son
Trevor are standing at the right.

mother's country; but neither Edwin nor any of the artists had ever been there. It was to be an important trip. Edwin's brother, Otto, also decided to go, and several relatives and friends joined the party. They were going to travel on horses and camels, but the drawback was that the only ones with money were Edwin and Otto. They bought up large supplies of food and planned to stay away for five weeks. However, by the time they got away from the mission there were more than a dozen in the party and long before they reached Ayers Rock the supplies had all been eaten. The visitors were not keen to live on bush tucker alone, so the party had to return to Hermannsburg without getting to their destination. Edwin was crestfallen when he returned. Until he has more experience, and is prepared to take only one or two men with him, long trips are off.

Like most aborigines Edwin is musical, and after one month's lessons on an organ could play hymn tunes in four parts. He is the only one of this group of native artists who has had a trip to a city. He was in Adelaide in 1946 on his way to Victoria to compete at Stawell and, during that period of six weeks, lived with white people. Since his return, however, he has made no attempt to improve his own living conditions or to break away from the very primitive ones of his people, although he has several hundreds of pounds saved and wants to build a more permanent dwelling as soon as he can procure suitable building materials. When there is a large native population—as at Hermannsburg—living under primitive conditions, it is very difficult for an odd family, surrounded by poor people who have nothing, to improve its home. Albert Namatjira built two houses at Hermannsburg and tried to improve his living conditions; but he is troubled by his relatives' and friends' inability to appreciate such things. Moreover, certain tribal customs show no respect for an individual's property.

IV

OTTO PAREROULTJA

*

OTTO PAREROULTJA, another pure-blood aboriginal, was born at Hermannsburg on 24th March 1914, and is the eldest of the three artist brothers. His wife, Kekoman, a pure-blooded aboriginal, is fair-haired and extremely good-looking. They have three young children, the eldest being Trevor, a very bright boy who was born on 17th January 1941.

Otto is not as robust as his brother Edwin, and is quite different in temperament, being of the dreamer-thinker type. Otto is very quiet and pleasant-natured; he never causes strife and is probably the best-liked man of the group.

Otto Pareroultja has been interested in painting since 1940. He is a true artist, full of character. He is not as brilliant or as quick a thinker as Edwin but, because of his love for painting and his perseverance, he has, over a number of years, worked out his own style, which is the most original and at the same time the most aboriginal in outlook among the group of aboriginal artists.

Although he began painting some years before Edwin, he seemed unable to progress beyond a certain point. He has always been true to his nature and for a few years most of his pictures were nocturnes. His paintings lacked colour. Although in his early days he did not receive much encouragement, he always kept coming back to his art. Before Edwin got a start, Albert set the standard and, although Otto showed the qualities of an artist, his unusual style was not appreciated. When Edwin had been painting a couple of years and I felt that he had established himself as an artist with a future, I said to him that it was a pity that his brothers Otto and Reuben were not doing more work. At this time they were not doing very much, although they had started to paint before Edwin, probably because of lack of encouragement and because they did not know if they were on the right lines in trying to do something according to their own outlook. Edwin talked with his brothers about the way I had encouraged him to paint in his own manner and had helped him sell his pictures. This must have made an impression, because soon after that both Otto and Reuben started bringing their paintings to me. They made so much advance that, although I had booked a date for Edwin to hold his first exhibition, I seriously considered holding a joint exhibition of the water-colours of the three Pareroultja brothers. However, I decided to keep to my original plan.

Otto went on and made a remarkable advance and developed a definite style of his own. He makes more use of shadows in his pictures than most artists. In fact, he developed decided aboriginal qualities in his work by making some of his shadows like aboriginal rock-drawings. I am sure this tendency was purely unconscious, brought about by his dreaming and his unspoilt attitude towards art. I have always encouraged Otto on the same lines as I have Edwin—telling him not to copy any other artist but to paint things the way he sees them and, above all, to be true to himself. Otto has had no help beyond that. At times when I have seen faces and forms worked into Otto's paintings and have asked him if he put them into his pictures on purpose, he has said that they were in the landscape as he had painted it. He goes back unconsciously into his own tribal mythology. The Arunta people are permitted by tradition to draw only concentric circles and wavy lines, such as they have on their sacred churungas. Otto has developed this symbolism in his work and made it a style of his own (Plate XII). Here the rocks, mountains, and trees are faithfully and well drawn, but the symbolism of circles and wavy lines is carried right through them without detracting from the picture, to which they give a primitive or aboriginal quality. Mr T. G. H. Strehlow, of the Adelaide University, who has the best knowledge of the Arunta tribe, and who is the authority on its language, literature, and music, says that of all the Australian aboriginal tribes that he knows the Arunta has the most ornamentation in its literature, art and music and that the music is full of rhythm. Some of the chants have up to thirteen beats to the bar.

The strongest feature in Otto's paintings is his rhythm or ornamentation (Plate X). Nothing quite like this painting has ever been done before. It is rhythmic and decorative from beginning to end, yet it portrays a real scene and was painted from nature. The famous Van Gogh never produced anything more complete with movement than this picture. And Otto, by the way, knows nothing about Van Gogh or his work.

There is another remarkable painting by Otto Pareroultja, full of rhythm (Plate XI). It almost looks like a red hot coal with flames and smoke belching from it; but it is painted from a real scene and is faithful in colour and form.

This aboriginal has something new to say and is a true artist who loves his work. In his own quiet way he will go on in his art because there are no limits for a man who has worked out his own style and way of seeing things. He has no inhibitions; his greatest asset is that he is himself and his paintings are a reflection of his own personality and background. Many who are familiar with the group of Arunta artists think that Otto will be the greatest of them. If he has the chance to continue, there is no limit to his possibilities.

[27

Otto held his first exhibition in Melbourne at the Athenaeum Art Gallery in December 1947, when his whole collection of forty-eight water-colours was sold. There was no wild rush to buy his pictures; but the public found that his work grew on them on acquaintance and they kept coming back to it and for it. This is the best recommendation for any picture. The most exacting test of good art is—can you live with it? Otto Pareroultja's work has the qualities necessary to fulfil this test.

Otto's next exhibition was held in Sydney at Anthony Horden's Art Galleries in November 1948. This exhibition was also most successful, the reaction of the public being the same as in Melbourne.

In 1947 the Arunta tribe at Hermannsburg presented to H.R.H. Princess Elizabeth on her twenty-first birthday, three water-colours painted by three of their fellow tribesmen—Albert Namatjira, Edwin Pareroultja and Otto Pareroultja—which were typical examples of these three artists' work. Although they are painting in similar country, they see it differently and have developed their own styles of painting. Because of this there is a place for them all from an economic point of view, since there are different tastes in art. Having three such artists in this group of Australian aborigines makes the art movement much more important and interesting and also shows what latent talent has been hidden in this hitherto despised race.

Otto was educated at the mission school at Hermannsburg, where, like his fellows, he learnt to read and write in the Arunta language. Australian aborigines could not do this before white men came to the country; and the reason they can be taught at Hermannsburg is that early missionaries went to the trouble to learn the Arunta language. Arunta is one of the few native languages that have been translated into English, and is the only one of which a complete grammar has been published. It was compiled by Mr T. G. H. Strehlow, who has written the foreword to this book.

At the mission school the natives also learn English and other general subjects; but there is no higher education, which is a great disadvantage to those who are ambitious to improve their position and to move among the white population.

Since leaving school, Otto has spent most of his time doing different types of work at the mission; he has always been a good reliable worker, whether as a stockman, shearer, carpenter, or gardener. At times he has relieved the native evangelist at Alice Springs. For some years he has been one of the members of the native council at Hermannsburg which supervises the discipline of the mission.

I have been out on painting trips with Otto, using camels for transport. On one of these trips, in August 1947, we camped on the bank of the Finke River at Glen Helen in the Macdonnell Range. Otto had with him his young son, Trevor, who thoroughly enjoyed the trip although we were away for more than five weeks and during that time had a most unusual experience for that season of the year—eight inches of rain fell in three weeks. The Finke River came down in flood and remained so for several weeks. Since we were on the north side of the Finke Gorge at Glen Helen, which we had traversed before the flood, we were cut off in all directions. Fortunately we were able to take shelter in the deserted Glen Helen homestead. Mr Bryan Bowman, the owner, who uses the home occasionally, had told me I could use the place if I wanted to paint near there. During all this time we were unable to get supplies and at last had to move for Hermannsburg. Since the river was still in flood it was impossible to get our camel team through the Gorge or over the Range, so we had to travel an extra forty miles, twenty miles west to a dry gap and twenty miles back to get to the south side of the Gorge where we had camped.

V

REUBEN PAREROULTJA

*

REUBEN PAREROULTJA was born at Hermannsburg on 3rd May 1916. Like his brothers Edwin and Otto, he is a pure-blood. They are the sons of Kristian and Auguste, and Pareroultja is Kristian's tribal name. It is not the aboriginal custom for sons to take their father's name, but in this case the white man's custom has been followed, and no doubt Pareroultja will remain the family name. Reuben's wife's name is Elsie and they have three young children.

Reuben went to the mission school and after leaving school worked at the mission. Since he has been married, he has lived for long periods with his wife's people west of Hermannsburg on the aboriginal reserve. This is rather a pity, because Reuben has too much ability to waste his time out on the reserve, where he gets small opportunity to make the best use of his talents. Bush tucker, moreover, does not agree with Reuben, who is a delicate person and needs the extra food he is able to get at the mission.

During 1942 and 1943 Reuben was in the aboriginal labour gang attached to the Army in Alice Springs, receiving five shillings a week and his keep. In 1943 he was discharged from the labour gang as being medically unfit. He returned to Hermannsburg and started to paint; but after a time went back to the reserve and did not do much painting until 1945. From then on he made rapid progress, especially when he came under the same system of encouragement and protection as Edwin and Otto, and sold a quantity of work locally at moderate prices. Like his brothers, he was able to develop a style that showed his own character and personality. Reuben is refined in nature, and delicate. During 1948 he did no painting because of poor health, and I am very concerned about his future. It is difficult to build up these natives in health when they have a long illness, mainly because of their living conditions. Their own relations do not know how to look after their sick. They show plenty of sympathy— too much at times—but often, when special food is given to build up a weak patient, the relations eat most of it. Fortunately Reuben had banked money from the sale of his pictures and during the whole of 1948 was able to live on his savings; but unless he is able to start work soon, he will have nothing left.

Much of Reuben Pareroultja's work shows his delicate nature (Plate XIII). He is a very good draughtsman and among the aboriginal artists he is the best at drawing animals. It is marvellous the movement he gets into them. One memorable picture he painted represents the bringing-in of the killer bullocks. One of the bullocks was lame and the horse was almost exhausted, and these things are depicted with telling veracity. Another very fine picture that went to Professor L. A. Mander, in America, showed a man with two camels; the relaxed movement of the camels as they lifted their feet was a remarkable piece of observation. It is very difficult to get the Arunta men to draw animals, especially their own native animals, because of the tribal law which forbids them to do it. They will do this only to please a white person. Because of Reuben's ability in drawing animals I had hoped he would specialize in them, for I felt that with so many artists in this group painting landscapes there was a good field for an animal painter amongst them. However, for some time now I have given up the idea of trying to force Reuben; it is impossible to make these people do things they are not interested in.

Only three of the group—Albert Namatjira, Edwin Pareroultja, and Otto Pareroultja—have held official one-man exhibitions of their paintings. It is felt that this is sufficient at this stage and up to the present it has not been considered wise to hold a group exhibition. Nor has it been considered wise to hold a group exhibition of the three Pareroultja artist brothers, although an exhibition of such quality and variety by three aboriginal brothers would be unique.

The Films Division of the Department of Information saw possibilities in a colour-film on the life and art of the three Pareroultja brothers. After the film *Namatjira the Painter* was made in 1946, Lee Robinson, as director, and Axel Poignant, photographer, returned to Hermannsburg and worked for some time on this film, and also camped with me at the Ormiston Gorge in the Macdonnell Range while I was on a painting trip there with the three Pareroultja brothers.

Reuben has outstanding qualities as a leader, although he shows it in a natural, quiet way. Considering his background he is the most emotionally refined aboriginal I know.

Reuben showed his sensitive feeling at the funeral of a brother-in-law who died in 1948. He left his sick-bed to pay his last respects and took charge of the mourners in his own quiet way, first of all removing the children, who usually sit around the open grave during a burial service in the mission cemetery. He then went away and brought his widowed sister, Monica, tenderly leading her on his arm, and placed her on the ground alongside the grave. He then brought his own mother in the same sympathetic manner and put her down near the grave. He then settled other relations close around. I had never seen this done before and one did not expect to see it. After the service there was another surprise as Reuben brought along in the same order, his widowed sister, then his mother and relations, and introduced them

[31

to the white people who attended the funeral, whom he thanked at the same time for their presence at the burial of his brother-in-law.

Before he became ill Reuben assisted at the mission school for a year or so, mainly looking after the children while they were out of school between special teaching periods and at meal-times.

VI

WALTER EBATARINJA

*

WALTER EBATARINJA is the only one of the group of artists who is not pure-blooded. He was born at Hermannsburg on 20th October 1915, and is the son of Joshua, a pure-blooded aboriginal, and Ruth, a half-caste. Walter is married to Kordula, a pure-blooded aboriginal, and they have seven children. Ebatarinja is probably taken from the name of Walter's father's father Ipitarinja, who was a honey-ant man and whose name signified "a dweller in a hollow".

Walter's father was the headman of the Hermannsburg group of the Arunta tribe; his father before him was also the headman and so on. This seems to give the lie to the theory put forward by anthropologists that the Australian aborigines have no kings or chiefs. Although Walter is not the eldest son, who would be the logical leader of his tribal group, he has made capital out of his inheritance. Jonathan, Albert Namatjira's father, came from the Mount Zeil country, which is about fifty miles north-west of Hermannsburg, and married a girl from the Hermannsburg tribal group, so he did not have any authority from a tribal point of view at Hermannsburg. When Albert became a successful artist and a man of means, Walter felt that Albert should help him because of his superior local tribal ancestry. Walter had ambitions to become an artist, so Albert had to teach him and also clothe and feed him, and this went on for two or three years.

Walter is Albert's leading pupil. Some others no doubt had assistance from him but not to the same extent; Walter had preference even over Albert's two eldest sons, Enos and Oskar, who started to paint at about the same time. Because of his blue blood, Walter demanded that; and Albert's two sons had to stand back and do the best they could for themselves. Naturally Walter made more rapid progress than Albert's sons, so that his work attracted quite a lot of attention at the mission and he had a ready sale for his pictures at moderate prices.

There is no doubt that Walter is clever. He has painted some very fine water-colours in the Albert Namatjira manner, yet they have not the quality or finish of Albert's work, and to me they always seem a bit empty. For Walter, technique was of first importance, as it always is with a copyist: the man who is prepared to copy another artist can imitate only the surface and does not know the thoughts and has not the soul of the original artist.

Walter's background is much the same as that of the other artists in this group. After leaving the mission school, he worked at different occupations on the mission. Walter excelled at stockwhip and belt plaiting and was making quite a fair income from this before he started painting.

Walter's breeding is most interesting. Hermannsburg is a wonderful field for the study of the mixture of white blood with the aboriginal. The older natives are mostly pure-blooded aborigines and there are a few half-caste women who have married pure-blooded men. Most of these had large families and their children have gone on marrying into other families and the tendency is for the white blood to be bred out again, as in Walter's family, his wife being pure-blooded. It is my experience among half-castes who have a white father and aboriginal mother—the usual order in Australia—that the girls are more reliable and more industrious than their brothers. When these half-caste girls marry pure-blooded aborigines, the order is reversed in their children and the boys are more reliable and hard-working than the girls. This conforms to Mendelism. At Hermannsburg, apart from the group of artists, a great majority of the key-men at the mission are of this blood mixture—sons of half-caste mothers and pure-blooded aboriginal fathers and they have more ambition than the average pure-blooded aborigines. Usually they are more reliable and as a rule do not tire of their work so easily, although they are probably more cunning and not so pleasant in nature. On the other hand, their sisters, while quite clever, are very lazy. The better working qualities and ambitions of the white man are handed down through the half-caste woman to her sons. These men, when they are living in an aboriginal community, as at Hermannsburg, appear to be more reliable than the half-caste man. At the same time they do not suffer from the complexes of the half-caste and are not worried about their colour.

Walter, with his white blood, does not lack in brains and is more cunning and probably more ambitious than the pure-blooded artists; but I feel that he lacks their originality. This may be brought about by his cunning and ambition. Because of Albert Namatjira's success, he naturally would want to imitate his work; but, when Edwin Pareroultja had recognition and success as an artist, Walter altered his style and followed Edwin for a while. The same thing happened when Otto Pareroultja was successful. Thus Walter has altered his style quite a lot since he painted the picture shown in Plate XV in 1945 under the influence of Albert Namatjira. It is difficult to say where Walter will end with his art. I feel that his touch of white blood has been a hindrance instead of a help, although there is no doubt he has great ability as a craftsman.

VII

ENOS AND OSKAR NAMATJIRA

*

ALBERT'S SONS, Enos and Oskar Namatjira, were born at Hermannsburg, Enos in 1920 and Oskar in 1922. These are Albert's two eldest children. Both are tall, and Oskar, who is powerfully built for a pure-blooded aboriginal, is probably the strongest native at Hermannsburg at present. He usually wins the shot putt when any sporting events are held at the mission. Enos and Oskar are both married. Enos lost his first wife a year or two ago and also lost his eldest boy, aged eight, at the end of 1948.

The background of the two men is much the same. Both went to the mission school and then worked at various jobs on the mission. Both served for about three years in the aboriginal labour gang which was attached to the Army in Alice Springs during the war. They painted on boomerangs for a living before they began painting in water-colours.

One main difference in the life of these two compared with that of the other young men at the mission was that they had a rich father. For some years this had the same effect on them as it has on white sons of wealthy fathers, who sometimes lack ambition and the will to work. "Why should I work when I have a rich father?" they said.

Both Enos and Oskar were very dissatisfied at times because their father did not give them as much as they wished. Albert did not always have a free hand, since he had other tribal relations who demanded help. In addition, some very distant tribesmen, such as Walter Ebatarinja, claimed assistance because of position in the tribe. When Albert bought his motor-truck, Enos was his first truck driver until he got out of hand and wasted so much of Albert's petrol that his father was forced to change to Oskar. Oskar did a better job, but he in the end also became difficult, and for the last year or so Albert has not used his truck and—strange but true—Albert, Enos and Oskar have all painted more and better pictures.

Both Enos and Oskar were too close to Albert not to be influenced by his outlook and his style of painting, although they did not get the help that Walter Ebatarinja had. It was in 1945 that Enos started to paint seriously in water-colours.

A water-colour painted towards the end of 1945 is reproduced in this book (Plate XVI). It definitely shows the influence of Albert and is quite a good example of Enos's work at that period. Since then Enos has altered his style a good deal, and shows much more originality in his latest work. The reason for this is that during the last couple of years Enos has been living out on the Aboriginal Reserve west of Hermannsburg, away from Albert's influence. The success of the Pareroultja brothers with their individual style of painting has given him more confidence in himself.

Oskar Namatjira began painting a little later than Enos and by 1945 was turning out good water-colours after the style of his father. During the period when Oskar was driving the truck he did very little painting; he said he hadn't the time. He was on the road most of the time during 1947. This was the year that Albert paid nearly £400 for fuel and repairs for his truck, while Oskar and his relations were having a glorious time. Albert would be taken to a good painting spot and left with some supplies, while Oskar with a truck-load of natives would travel round the country, visiting different camps of aborigines, and such places as Haast Bluff, Areyonga, Hermannsburg, Jay Creek, and Alice Springs. Albert did not get much benefit from his truck, but his relations and their relatives enjoyed themselves to the full. They no doubt felt that Albert had unlimited money. If that ran out, he would only have to paint a few more pictures and sell them at high prices. Albert could not object while he had the money to pay for all this, since what he had belonged to his relations as much as to himself. The only way for it to stop was for Albert to get tired of work; but Albert was an exceptional aboriginal who did not get tired of work. Still, the best of good things can't go on for ever. Albert's bank account had dwindled and the truck had had such a belting on the rough bush tracks that it had to be put away until there were funds enough to give it a thorough overhaul. Oskar lost his job and went back to painting, and quite a number of Albert's relations were looking for a job the following Monday morning when work was given out at the mission.

Since this orgy of spending, Oskar has settled down to do some very good painting. He began in the style of his father; but after a while his work seemed to be influenced by that of Otto Pareroultja. At present he is painting in his father's style again, particularly in that of his earlier paintings. During the last year Oskar has done a lot of work and is one of the most improved painters of the group.

Enos and Oskar still think their father should do something for them. A few years ago they wanted him to buy a couple of hundred head of cows for them, so that they might become pastoralists on the Aboriginal Reserve at Undandita. Albert felt it was his duty to give his sons a start and even asked the Director of Native Affairs for permission to run the cattle on the Reserve. This was not granted, as it was felt that it would not be fair to the other natives for Albert to become a station owner on the Aboriginal Reserve. Albert is never beaten; he is a slow but deep thinker who has a lot of reasoning power. Now his latest idea, and quite a sound one, is that he wants to get a block of Crown land near the Aboriginal Reserve. He has already spoken to Native Affairs officers and Lands Department officers and he feels that they have given him enough encouragement to press for a block. His idea is to get this block in his own name, and that his two eldest sons, Enos and Oskar, should work it, and that it should go to the family when he is dead. There are certain regulations in regard to the number of cattle one must have and Albert feels that he can comply with these. Albert should be encouraged in the venture for there is no reason why these men should not have a chance, since they are good stockmen and know the country and conditions. Of course Albert will have a lot of worry if he gets a block; but it may be a long time, if ever, before another pure-blooded aboriginal will be in a position to try such an interesting experiment as this. The Government spends an enormous amount of money on the aborigines and this would cost them nothing except approval.

VIII

HENOCH RABERABA

*

HENOCH RABERABA, a pure-blooded aboriginal, was born at Hermannsburg on 16th July 1914, and is married to Regina, also pure-blooded. They have three children. The Arunta meaning of "raberaba", which should be spelt "rubaruba", is "willy-willy", which is a whirlwind. It is interesting to find that Henoch is in the same tribal group, "Kuguarea", as Albert Namatjira and Edwin, Otto, and Reuben Pareroultja. Thus five of the same marriage class are in this group of ten artists.*

Henoch has a background similar to that of the other artists of this group. Like them, he went to the mission school, and after leaving school worked on the mission at different occupations. He was particularly interested in stock work and was a good stockman, experienced in handling cattle, sheep, horses, camels, donkeys and goats.

When the Hermannsburg Aboriginal Pastoralists' Scheme began in 1944, Henoch was one of the four original members who were set going with fifty cows, a bull, stock horses, and gear, free of interest, the principal to be paid back when they had their sales of fat bullocks. They were also advanced rations up to the value of ten shillings a week and could collect these at the Areyonga Ration Depot. At Areyonga a cash store is run by the mission to enable the aborigines who have skins, money, or curios to trade them for cash or goods. The idea of the cash or barter store was to encourage the aborigines to stay on the reserve and not to go to the towns. The store enabled them to satisfy their desire for a few extras to relieve the monotony of bush tucker. They therefore had no need to look for white man's food, which was the main attraction. These aboriginal pastoralists were allowed to run their cattle on the Areyonga Aboriginal Reserve.

Henoch has always shown plenty of ability. But he has usually tired of his jobs,

* There are eight marriage sections in the Arunta tribe. Albert's three artist sons, Enos, Oskar, and Ewald, are in a different section from their father. It is remarkable how closely related this group of artists are. Walter Ebatarinja is also related to Albert. This only leaves Richard Moketarinja who is not closely related, although he, too, would be distantly related. Time will prove if this big art development is just an outstanding quality of this closely related group of Arunta men, or if it is one of the important characteristics of the Australian aboriginal.

this being a weakness of the Australian aboriginal. The aboriginal pastoralists would have to wait at least three years before having suitable cattle of their own rearing for sale. After remaining for two years as a pastoralist on the reserve, Henoch lost interest in being a stockman and asked to be relieved of his commitments. Two other aborigines were prepared to take over Henoch's assets as a going concern. This was finally arranged by the Hermannsburg Aboriginal Pastoralist Council and Henoch was freed.

Henoch went back to the mission at Hermannsburg and soon showed interest in the new art movement. I recall that some years previously he had expressed his desire to paint and I had given him some painting materials; but he did not continue and I had thought he would not have enough interest to stick at painting. I also felt that he was of a restless nature, as his experience as a pastoralist appeared to show. With more age and experience of life, he has probably found that art is his natural bent.

Towards the end of 1946 Henoch went out on a month's painting trip with Albert Namatjira. When Albert returned to the mission to work on the film *Namatjira the Painter* he told me that Henoch had three water-colours in which I might be interested. I showed these paintings to the members of the party who were making the film and they bought all three.

This first sale inspired Henoch, who has devoted all his time since then to painting. He has sold his work at moderate prices. During 1947 he painted and sold more water-colours than any artist in this group. After Henoch's first month with Albert Namatjira, when he painted in Albert's manner, he spent a few weeks with Edwin Pareroultja, another tribal brother, and then brought in work similar to Edwin's. Since then he seems to have worked out a style of his own which lies between those of Albert Namatjira and Edwin Pareroultja. By the time Henoch had been painting for three months he was turning out work which showed a very good colour sense, good drawing, and remarkable technical skill for a man of such little experience.*

It appears that at last Henoch has found his right occupation in life; but it is a big jump from aboriginal stockman to water-colour artist. Because of Henoch's past I have been slow to form an opinion on his work. I have been waiting to see how he continues to develop in his art. I have always felt that Henoch lacked the solidity of character to be a great artist; but when one comes to examine his latest work one cannot deny his ability (Plate XVIII). This shows beautiful colour, a wonderful sense of decoration, and strong drawing, while the workmanship and quality are amazing for a man who has been painting for only two years, a pure-blooded aboriginal who has seen only the work done in his own locality. If Henoch can improve, he will create for himself an important place as an artist.

* It is amazing how these men take to water-colours; the technical problems of the medium don't seem to worry them.

IX

RICHARD MOKETARINJA

*

RICHARD MOKETARINJA, who is a pure-blooded aboriginal, was born near Hermannsburg in 1916. He is married to Nabitji, also pure-blooded. They have two children.
"Moketarinja" means a snake curled up in a circle.

Richard attended the mission school and later worked on the mission. As a youth
he was rather wild and difficult to handle at times, and used to be in a lot of fights.
He even had a few brushes with white members of the mission staff. In 1936 he was the
champion runner at Hermannsburg. He has always shown a lot of character and
because of this some people found him difficult to manage. In reality that only
showed he had a mind of his own. When he has worked with any white employer
who understood him, he has been a very good and intelligent worker. Mr G. A.
Drogemuller, who has built a number of buildings at Hermannsburg, Alice Springs,
Haast Bluff, and Areyonga for the Finke River mission during the past few years,
always considered Richard one of his best men on all types of building work.
Richard's weakness was that his restless nature craved change.

In 1942 he was making several pounds a week by painting on boomerangs, but
volunteered to join the aboriginal labour gang with the Army at Alice Springs to
earn five shillings a week. He got experience, but soon realized it was not a good
business proposition. Nevertheless, he stayed with the Army for three years.

It was in 1940 that I first became interested in Richard as an artist who showed
outstanding drawing ability. I took him out with me on a painting trip when I
travelled with camels for more than a month, painting at the Finke Gorge, Glen
Helen, and Ormiston Gorge, Macdonnell Range. I used with Richard my method of
encouragement without teaching. On this trip he painted some good water-colours
which showed a lot of original primitive quality.

In 1941 I took Richard out on a longer trip, when I also had Albert Namatjira
with me. We travelled on camels to Hamilton Downs Station, Jay Fish Hole, Standly
Chasm, and Jay Creek. We were away for nearly two months on this painting
trip.

Ghost Gum, Ormiston Gorge, Macdonnell Range. Mount Sonder
and Mount Teil can be seen in the distance.

Albert Namatjira's three artist sons, Enos on the dark horse,
Ewald on the white horse, and Oskar standing.

On this trip I wanted Richard to paint in his own way. He may have been too young or there may have been some tribal reason, for Richard and his people were not ready for self-expression at that stage. Apart from the period when he was decorating boomerangs Richard did not take to painting seriously until a couple of years ago.

Again I am forced to realize the importance of the breakaway by Edwin Pareroultja. Undoubtedly his success has opened the way to several of the more original native artists.

Early in 1947 Richard Moketarinja painted a few water-colours in a very primitive manner, the most interesting feature being his stress on parallelism, which is a very early form of primitive art. (In the literary field, for example, the Psalms of David show a lot of parallelism.) As Richard was considered a valuable worker on the mission, he got little encouragement for his primitive paintings at this period. In 1948 the urge to paint came uppermost and he spent the whole year painting. Of the Hermannsburg artists he improved most during 1948. He also probably painted the most pictures in that year and had good sales at low prices.

Of all the Arunta artists he has the most primitive sense of design. Since he has gained more confidence in his work and acquired more technical ability, his sense of decoration has become richer and he has risen above mere parallelism. For a man with such a primitive mind, his drawing is amazing; even when drawing mechanical objects, he is one of the outstanding draughtsmen of the group. His character is showing up in his work. Because of his strength, he is giving us an entirely new outlook on the landscape of his own country. Because of his originality and force of character he is not likely to be influenced by other artists. Richard Moketarinja has taken a long time to think over things since he first started painting in 1940. If Richard had wanted to imitate, he would have done it before this, because he knew the value that was put on Albert Namatjira's paintings.

A painting of Mount Giles, Macdonnell Range, done in the winter of 1948, shows a lot of originality (Plate XIX). It is full of decoration, colour, good drawing, and quality. It is interesting to see how flatly Moketarinja has treated the gum-tree in a primitive manner which helps its decorative quality. That would make it a suitable design for textiles.

The water-colour of Palm Valley, James Range, was painted towards the end of 1948 (Plate XX). It is a very advanced piece of painting, beautifully drawn, good in colour, with wonderful contrasts between the textures of the palms and the gum-trees. The whole picture shows amazing feeling for original and primitive decoration. It is essentially the work of an unspoilt artist, one who has the ability to draw well and a natural colour sense. Although the picture is painted from nature and is very true to the country, it is totally different from the work of Moketarinja's fellow artists. The difference is subtle, because all these men are painting the same country and so, if

[41

they are sincere, their paintings must show a lot of similarity to the untrained and uninitiated eye.

Apart from Moketarinja's ability, his originality and strength of character, although making him difficult at times, enable him to follow his own line of thought, so that he gets more feeling in his painting than the artist who must follow fashion because of the desire for popularity and success.

Richard's art history since 1940 bears this out. At times during those years he knew that he could make more money out of his art either by painting on boomerangs or water-colours than he could out of any other work. If the man had been a poor worker, he might have followed the usual easy way of the aborigines and lived on his relations. But, when Richard Moketarinja was quite satisfied that he could express himself and would be encouraged in his own original style of work, as in 1948, he put his whole energy into his painting. He has turned out an enormous amount, at the same time showing a steady progress in all departments of his art.

X

EWALD NAMATJIRA

*

EWALD NAMATJIRA, born at Hermannsburg on 11th July 1930, is also pure-blooded. He is the third son of Albert Namatjira and Rubena. Like his father and two elder brothers, Ewald has taken to art and is a natural water-colourist. He is the youngest of the group of Arunta artists and, because of his age, should not be pushed but allowed to paint when he feels the desire. The aborigines have a long youth and usually take a number of years to settle down or develop enough ambition to do something really worthwhile. Ewald is a true artist, who shows more promise of originality than either his father or his two elder brothers.

Ewald's life story is quite different from that of the other members of the group in that, until he started painting water-colours at the age of seventeen years, he was considered of no economic value by members of the staff at the mission. He is probably one of the best examples of our aboriginal youth problem. Often these youths are considered useless, yet as in Ewald's case, they may have a hidden talent of great importance.

When a child, Ewald was rather delicate and complained of headaches, especially when he had to go to school. The teacher of the mission school at Hermannsburg felt sorry for the boy, so Ewald was allowed to stay away when he had headaches. His father also felt that his boy was too ill to attend school. The result has been that Ewald has had no education and cannot even write his own name. Members of the mission staff even felt that he was subnormal. His father Albert was very fond of him, and used to take him out on his painting trips. The life suited Ewald. No doubt he learnt a lot of bushcraft and grew in strength; but he does not look as robust as his brothers.

When Ewald was old enough to work, he was employed on the mission at various jobs. After working for short periods, he would get tired and complain that he was unwell and unable to work. Because Ewald had got out of going to school in much the same way, the mission authorities felt that the boy was unsuited for anything, and so lost interest in him. If Ewald had been a white boy, he would have found it more difficult to get out of going to school or working; but as the present attitude towards our aborigines is that lack of education in them does not matter, he was allowed to start life as a man without even being able to read and write. To say he was a native does not excuse his lack of education. Because of their backwardness as a race education is really of more importance to them than it is to the white man.

When Ewald brought along his first water-colour painting in 1947, his work was not taken seriously; but at Hermannsburg anybody who shows artistic ability has an opportunity to put his work up for sale along with the other artists at the mission.

Ewald Namatjira showed quite a lot of originality and ability from the start. When he continued to show improvement along lines totally different from those of other artists, I told him to continue in his own way and, although he might go out on painting trips with his father, not to copy his father's style of work. I also talked to his father, urging him not to interfere with Ewald's style of painting. He said he could see what I meant and would let Ewald go his own way. This method has been a great success, for although Ewald lives much closer to his father than his brothers do, he has much more originality than either of them.

This originality is partly made possible by the breakaway by Edwin Pareroultja, in that Ewald has felt free and happy to express himself in paint in his own way. Ewald, especially since he had no schooling, would have found it very irksome to go to a painting school or to follow another artist. It was ideal for him that he could paint when he wished and in the manner he felt he should and at the same time have prospects of sales.

Ewald has painted some remarkable water-colours in the short time he has been painting. He continues to progress in his drawing, handling of the medium, sense of decoration, and atmospheric feeling. In the last two qualities he is stronger than his father. In fact he shows so much natural ability and originality and has improved so much in the very short time he has been painting that one is inclined to think he may be a genius with tremendous possibilities as an artist. Ewald does not turn out a great quantity of work; but I think that is all to the good considering his age. Although he paints quite a variety of subjects, he has a leaning for clouds with rain falling out of them (Plate XXI). This is a recent picture and is a wonderful piece of observation and painting. Apart from the beautifully drawn ironwood-tree, the mountain and cloud shadows cast on it, with rain falling, give a feeling that the country is really wet. This picture grows on one because it is so full of lively feeling. It is remarkable that a boy who has had no lessons in painting and no education according to our standards, could have painted a picture so sensitive and so full of quality. But, of course, you will remember that, instead of going to school, Ewald would go out on painting trips with his father. Besides learning his bushcraft, he observed life and the country, its elements and atmosphere. No doubt he has picked up a lot from his famous father by seeing

Walter Ebatarinja sketching at Hermannsburg.

Aboriginal children making drawings. Even these primitive
children have a flair for art.

him at work; also they would talk about the paintings as they sat around their camp-fire at night.

From the reproduction of Ewald's work one may get the impression that he is following his father. The painting has some of the finish that Albert achieves, but one needs to see several pictures by the artist to give a real opinion. Ewald has a different outlook from his father, with different qualities. He is interested in different subject matter. He is also much more sensitive, and his paintings are influenced more by his own feelings than Albert Namatjira's are. I would say that Ewald is more influenced by the weather than are any of the Arunta artists, and his sensitive nature enables him to record this on paper. Aborigines are children of Nature, and there is no doubt that this is a true child.

It will be interesting to see how Ewald Namatjira will develop in view of his limited background. Even if he does not advance any farther, he is now able to give something of lasting pleasure. For that reason alone I would not like to see him forced to produce large quantities of paintings. Mass production would be foreign to his nature.

In some ways Ewald is the most interesting of the aboriginal artists. Pastor Albrecht, who has been superintendent of the mission at Hermannsburg for the past twenty-three years and is recognized as a leading authority on the Australian aborigines, was amazed when he saw one of Ewald's paintings recently. "To think this boy is useless, yet can paint a picture like that just because a door has been opened to him!" were his words.

This opens up a new field. We have all heard how useless the Australian aboriginal is and that it is only a waste of time and money to try to help him help himself. Have we been taking the right attitude towards them? The usual policy is for the Government to hand out a few miserable rations. This tends to make the people mere beggars—the dole was never any good to any race of people. In the case of the aborigines, one of the greatest faults in the past has been the handing out of government rations, mostly at police stations and in towns. They have been seduced from their own bush country, which they understood, and where they were able to eke out an existence. When they got the rations, they felt they were made; but these rations were not a complete diet, although the natives were ignorant of that. The Government felt they had done their duty and there the story ended.

On the other hand, most missions sent out missionaries into the field who were imbued with the idea of making Christians of these primitive people. The missionaries were, in most cases, trained only in theology and apart from that were sometimes unsuited for the task. If the Government and the missions are sincere, they should co-operate to work out a plan by which they can really help the aborigines, who are much better left alone unless the job is thoroughly and whole-heartedly done. I feel, if we intend to help them, we should be honest and make our

[45

effort genuine and wholehearted. If we think we have a higher civilization and can be of benefit to them, we should be prepared to give them the same chances as our own white people. In the past we have lost their confidence by making ourselves their friends yet failing to go the full distance. The natives make no secret of their recognition of this fact when they see the third-class help that is offered to them. Naturally, they make little response, since they feel they are not wanted in our civilization.

Take Ewald as an object lesson. Here was a boy playing the white man's game of make-believe. As I see him at present, he is no fool. He was too lazy—or clever—to go to school and to work; but when he saw a door opened to him, he had the ability and the brains to enter. There must be fields, apart from art, that others are interested in. Surely there are white people in all walks of life who have the ability, patience and desire to help the natives. Just anything is not good enough for them. Because they are backward is all the more reason why we should use the best brains available to help them.

XI

SUMMING UP AND FUTURE

*

IN 1947 Gordon B. Hempstead, an American author, spent several months in Australia. When I met him one evening in Alice Springs he questioned me for four hours, wanting to know why the art movement had taken place in Central Australia. A couple of months later, when I was in Sydney at Edwin Pareroultja's exhibition, Hempstead called in before leaving for home. His last words were, "I still have no answer to my question why this art movement started in Central Australia amongst the so-called lowest primitive race in the world. . . . There's nothing like this movement among any other aboriginal race in the world," he added. "We have nothing like it in the States!"

Hempstead had counters to all my answers; but I still think it was a combination of circumstances which enabled the development to take place. The first question I will try to answer is concerned with the people themselves. Let us call the Arunta people a desert tribe. Nobody can definitely say where they came from; but there's no doubt they derived from a higher civilization. They probably came down through India on their way to Australia.

There seem to have been at least two different waves of these original inhabitants of Australia. One would naturally think the tribes living in the desert in the heart of Australia when the white man first settled in the country, were the purest in blood, even if they were not the first race to inhabit this continent. There is no doubt they have been isolated for a longer period than the coastal tribes: that is proved by the difference in their customs.

The most remarkable difference is that the Central Australian tribes are the only people who used the stone churunga. This is the most highly prized article any of the Australian tribes possessed, and the Arunta district was the main home of the stone tjurungas. The symbolical carvings on the stones are a practice of desert tribes, the nearest parallel being the early Egyptian hieroglyphics. The opinion is often expressed by people who have had experience with the central Australian, and also of the natives around the north coast of Australia, that the central Australian natives are of a much

[47

poorer type, physically and mentally, than are the coastal natives. However, Bill Harney, the author of *Taboo*, a book on the Australian aborigines, a man of wide experience and an admirer of the water-colours of Albert Namatjira, once told me that their art only strengthened the opinion he held that the desert tribes were cleverer than the coastal natives round Darwin. The reason he gave was that the coastal natives had a much easier life. Food was easy to find, and this tended to make the coastal native a pleasanter person. The desert native had a terrific struggle to exist which made him very cunning and difficult to handle. For that reason he was misjudged as dull. This seems quite a reasonable observation and, although I have had very little to do with natives of the north coast of Australia, I agree that the inland native, far from being dull, is probably a better judge of our character than we are of his.

The Australian aboriginal is famous for his bushcraft and ability as a tracker. To him the ground is an open book where the tracks of every walking and creeping thing are written on pages of sand and stone. Apart from that he knows the life history of every animal, bird, fish, insect, tree, and plant.

The Arunta artists are fortunate in that they are still living in their tribal country.* Before the white man came, very few of them would have been allowed to roam over all this country. They are in a unique position because of the mission country and the large aboriginal reserve which borders the western boundary of the mission. West of the aboriginal reserve are millions of acres of Crown land; although it is mostly desert, in good seasons they can wander over parts of this area.

The mission natives are not quite as expert in bushcraft as the more primitive tribes on the reserve; yet, because of this fortunate position, they are still good bushmen. They may also make contact with other, more primitive, tribes and are able to roam over this large area because of the peaceful influence of the mission. Additionally, they are living in the most "paintable" part of Australia and one of the most colourful in the world. Countries the size of Belgium or Holland could easily fit into this area.

The climate, too, is a help; first of all because there is a low rainfall—mostly under ten inches a year. Low rainfall is mainly responsible for the red sandhills, soil and rock, because there is enough rain to cause oxidation of the iron in the soil and rock, yet not enough to wash all the iron out. With the clear, dry atmosphere there are amazingly blue skies and a marvellous light which reflects the blue of the sky into the landscape, making beautiful distant blue mountains. Closer up, this blue reflected into the red rocks and gorges makes purple shadows of all shades and tones, while the foliage of trees is saturated with purples and blues, including subtle powder blues.

The winter climate is most invigorating. I am sure it has a big influence on the

* The mission property comprises nearly a million acres.

48]

native artists, for in the dry winter months they get sunshine which, with the cool climate, gives ideal painting conditions for six to eight months of the year.

Most of this country is about 2000 feet above sea level, so that the summer climate, although very hot in the daytime, is mostly cool at night. The climate in the Centre gives its natives an advantage over those living along the north coast of Australia, where the more humid conditions tend to make the inhabitants more easy-going and less ambitious.

A group of people like the Arunta artists, who have shown they are ambitious and can work well for themselves when they are interested, might find conditions less stimulating in the Darwin area, where people have an easier life.

I once had an interesting experience in 1941 in Central Australia, for which one could not blame the climate, although I think the same experience might be exaggerated by the climate near Darwin. I was on a painting trip with Albert Namatjira and Richard Moketarinja and we travelled on camels to Standly Chasm, which is on the boundary of the Jay Creek Aboriginal Reserve. On this reserve the Government has a ration depot where rations are handed out to all the natives, young or old, sick or strong, and nobody needs to give any service in return unless he wishes. This system only encourages laziness, most notably among the men, who were often too lazy even to go out hunting to supplement their poor meat ration. It was marvellous country for painting. Its majestic rock formations are of all shades of colour, particularly brilliant oranges and reds of amazing grandeur. Albert Namatjira, a mature native of experience, a man who knew what he wanted and knew also the value of his art, was not influenced by his proximity to the ration depot, where dozens of his fellow men were sitting around waiting for the next ration day. But to Richard Moketarinja, a young man, it was different. Richard had to get the camels every morning and bring them into our camp—this is the usual custom in a camel camp, even if one is having a prolonged stay as we were. The camels would be hobbled and let go every evening and would often wander on to the reserve and near the ration depot. When Richard found the camels anywhere near the depot, he would call in and spend the greater part of the day in that camp. Albert painted six good water-colours while we were at Standly Chasm camp. Richard painted one very small picture. When I questioned him, he told me the young men at the depot would tell him not to bother about work, but to sit down and talk, which is one of their favourite pastimes.

At Hermannsburg the artists are able to fight against the loafer influence, partly because at the mission the policy is, No rations for the able-bodied unless they work. I feel, however, that the climate also helps them.

The art development would never have taken place among these people if the Finke River mission, or some similar mission, had not been in existence. There is no doubt that without the work of the mission, the Arunta tribe would not have been in

[49

existence today. It would have been the old story of the Australian aborigines dying out. The country where Hermannsburg now stands would have been taken up by private people and turned into a cattle station. A few of the local natives would have remained to work on the station. The rest would have drifted to the towns and gradually died out. I doubt if among the aborigines living in Alice Springs at the present time there are any who belong to that country. Some have travelled hundreds of miles from the Petermann Range in Western Australia, while others have come from the far north. But the long history of the mission at Hermannsburg since 1877 until the present day has been the salvation of the Arunta tribe; through its teachings and guidance it has given these people a solidity that has made them the most famous of all the Australian aboriginal tribes.

Hermannsburg is also placed in a good pastoral position. Fortunately for the natives, the first missionaries arrived at Hermannsburg before all the good country was taken up for selection. The Arunta natives then were still unspoilt and living in their original tribal state. The growth of Alice Springs, eighty miles away, was so slow for the first sixty years that it gave the people a chance to adjust themselves to changing conditions and the mission was able to consolidate its position. This was reflected when more than thirty young men from Hermannsburg who served in the aboriginal labour gang with the Army in Alice Springs during the war, all returned to Hermannsburg and district when they were discharged from the Army.

After seventy years there are more Arunta people living at Hermannsburg than were there when the white man first came to the Centre. Although they have been influenced by missionaries and most of them have become Christians and do not practise all of their tribal customs, they are still encouraged to speak their own language. The New Testament has been translated into Arunta. Most of them also speak the Loritja language, which is totally different and is used by neighbouring tribes. They are also taught the English language in the mission school. They are encouraged to keep their tribal marriage laws, which they abide by. The tribe has a large tract of good hunting country, which they are free to roam over and so satisfy their walkabout instincts.

A complaint of station owners that mission natives are spoilt and consequently poor workers has some truth according to their standards. Most station owners employ only the best natives and try to keep the aboriginal camps on the station as small as possible and under these conditions it is possible to maintain fairly strict discipline. It is totally different on the mission stations. The missionaries bring Christianity and the brotherhood of man, and also try to educate the natives and teach them the value of money. Because of this policy they are unable to achieve the same result as the station owners who keep only the best workers. To the missionaries that would be against the teaching of Christianity. They have to put up with all types, the workers, and the loafers whom the private stations don't want; so, try as hard as

50]

they will, they are unable to turn out the type of aboriginal worker which most station owners desire.

On the other hand, an art movement among the aborigines on the cattle stations could never have developed as this one did at the mission at Hermannsburg. In the first place the aborigines working on the stations would have neither the initiative nor the pride to try such a venture. They would lack the organization to carry it out. At the mission the natives have had a freer hand and have developed because they have been encouraged to do things for themselves. The mission has been prepared to help the natives in their art movement and up to the last year or two the aboriginal artists at Hermannsburg received every penny their water-colours brought. As the business has grown to such volume and takes so much of the mission staff's time, it has been decided to take five per cent off sales. This goes into a fund that helps to pay for the running of the mission. The rest of the money is paid into the bank accounts of the different artists. Without an organization like a mission the aboriginal artists would have had no chance. They had not the experience or the business ability to do it for themselves and it is only an organization like a mission that would be prepared to give them the full benefit of their labours without exploitation in any way whatever.

Because the art movement has grown to such large proportions and is so important to the development of the aborigines, it is felt by the people at Hermannsburg who have the interests of the artists at heart, that the whole movement should be under some organization. As a result, three Councils or Committees have been formed, all members serving in an honorary capacity. There are two Advisory Committees, the Namatjira Arts Committee and the Pareroultja Arts Committee. Of the first the white members are Pastor S. O. Gross, Mr A. P. Latz, Miss H. Wurst, and Rex Battarbee, and the native artist members Albert Namatjira, Walter Ebatarinja, and Oskar Namatjira. The Pareroultja Arts Committee has for its white members Mr O. A. Wallent, Mrs A. P. Latz, Miss M. Kennedy, and Rex Battarbee, and its native artist members are Edwin Pareroultja, Otto Pareroultja, Reuben Pareroultja, Henoch Raberaba, Richard Moketarinja, Enos Namatjira, and Ewald Namatjira. These committees hold meetings to discuss any business matter dealing with the aboriginal artist members. All the pictures painted by artist members are handled by the respective committees and priced by them. The Committees also organize the exhibitions held by artist members. The senior Council is the Arunta Arts Council which deals with the larger issues. It watches over the interests of such of the aboriginal artists residing in the Hermannsburg district as have been admitted into membership. Such admittance is conditional upon recommendation by the existing Arts Committees. Members of the Arunta Arts Council are the Superintendent of the Finke River mission, who acts as Chairman, a resident of Alice Springs, and one member of each of the Arts Committees apart from Rex Battarbee who is also a member. A representative of the Native Affairs Branch is invited to attend meetings.

There are no aboriginal artists on this Council; but they have a non-artist aboriginal representative who at present is Manasse, one of the outstanding natives at the mission.

The aim of the Council and the Committees is to protect the artists by making the disposal of their pictures as foolproof as possible so that they may get the benefit of their work, and be enabled to save something for lean times and their old age. The business ability of the men is not as high as their artistic ability, and they are not in a position to look after their affairs. It is to be hoped that their experience on these Committees will enable them in time to manage their own affairs.

The art movement has to be viewed as a whole and for the benefit of the whole tribe, not just for one or two of the artists who may waste their money or cripple the whole movement. Through this art development the aborigines have a wonderful chance to re-establish themselves alongside the white population, for it is the first time that a group of Australian aborigines has shown such possibilities of establishing itself as a unit in our civilization. As I have said before, these artists are in a unique position as far as their country, climate, scenery, and isolation are concerned.

Mr T. G. H. Strehlow, in his book *Aranda Traditions*, says of these people's love of native soil: "The foregoing account explains in some measure the overwhelming affection felt by a native for his ancestral territory. Mountains and creeks and springs and water-holes are, to him, not merely interesting or beautiful scenic features in which his eyes may take a passing delight; they are the handiwork of ancestors from whom he himself has descended. He sees recorded in the surrounding landscape the ancient story of the lives and the deeds of the immortal beings whom he reveres; beings, who for a brief space may take on human shape once more; beings, many of whom he has known in his own experience as his fathers and grandfathers and brothers, and as his mothers and sisters. The whole countryside is his living, age-old family tree. The story of his own totemic ancestor is to the native the account of his own doings at the beginning of time, at the dim dawn of life, when the world as he knows it now was being shaped and moulded by all-powerful hands. He himself has played a part in that first glorious adventure, a part smaller or greater according to the original rank of the ancestor of whom he is the present reincarnated form."

If the natives are to survive as a group and be of any lasting benefit to their people, they must not go off to live in one of the large cities or be swallowed up in the mass of artistic thought and probably sidetracked and lost in the slums. Most aborigines, because of the colour bar and their primitive living habits, go to the slum areas, which become their graveyards. Australian history has proved this to be true. The Hermannsburg aboriginal artists have no need to do that, for, with the help of a few sympathetic white people, they have been able to continue their work up to this stage. There is no reason why this help cannot be continued until they are able to look after themselves.

One unfortunate gap in this art development is that because of the poor living

Richard Moketarinja at Hermannsburg with the mission church
in the background.

Henoch Raberaba about to mount one of his horses.

conditions of the artists they and their people have not been able to gain the full appreciation of their paintings which comes of living with them in their own homes. Because of their poverty they have been over-anxious to sell their pictures as quickly as possible; but now an effort is being made to avoid this and already some of the artists have given paintings towards a collection to form a Memorial Art Gallery at Hermannsburg. The collection will belong to the Arunta people as a lasting memorial, to show present and future generations what the artists have been able to do. It will also give the natives themselves a chance to study and appreciate those works of art which they are at present unable to enjoy because of their lack of housing. It is to be hoped that enough funds will be raised to erect a building suitable for an Art Gallery.

If the natives are able to preserve the mission areas and aboriginal reserves which at present are their right, they will have a permanent home, so that out of the art development they should be able to build up an art colony of their own. They could also add weaving and modelling to their arts. People will travel from all parts of the world to see them in their own surroundings, for, apart from their reputation as artists, they live in one of the most colourful parts of the world. For at least six months in the year, the climate is suitable for tourists. The country for two hundred miles east and west of Alice Springs could become the outstanding inland winter resort of Australia.

Oversea visitors will become more and more interested in this region because it is the real Australia. Coastal areas and cities are much the same all over the world; but, when the Centre of Australia with its marvellous dry sunny climate, its amazing blue and purple mountain ranges patterned by red gorges and cliffs and river valleys of many colours, becomes more accessible, people from all places will visit it and enjoy it. Already people from all walks of life have visited the Centre and, by being so impressed with its various charms, have proved its great future as a tourist resort, especially for the person who wants to see something different and to find nature in all its primitive grandeur.

Most people think Central Australia is mostly desert, flat and uninteresting but, apart from its mountain ranges, which are the highest in Australia except for the Australian Alps, it has a variety of trees and vegetation remarkable in form and colour. Of course the favourite tree is the ghost gum, which lends such wonderful contrast to the landscape, whether it is fighting for its existence in a crevice of red rock hundreds of feet above soil or water, or spreading itself in the rich soil of a mountain valley where its beautiful white limbs throw a tracery across the blue sky. Most visitors who have really seen this country come again, for there is something in the spell of the Inland which is difficult to explain but which gets into one's blood. The aboriginal artists will also attract people, as has already been proved by Albert Namatjira.

Apart from this art development, the Hermannsburg Aboriginal Pastoral Scheme is another reason for believing there is a great chance for at least some Australian aborigines to re-establish themselves. It has been proved that this scheme will work, providing there is sympathetic assistance to help the natives to control their business affairs until they are able to do so themselves. This may take generations; but it must be done. The Government should protect the aboriginal reserve and allow more aboriginal pastoralists to come into the scheme. Water should be stored on the Reserve.

So far all the artists and pastoralists are Arunta men; but in this area there are Loritja, Pintubi, Pitjentjara and Ngalia tribes who are still intact but living in a more primitive state than the Arunta people. Although these western tribes are backward, they are becoming interested in the success of the Arunta men. They, too, want to become artists and cattlemen. It is to be hoped they will also have their chance to show any ability or latent talent they may possess. Who knows but that some of these men may show us a new form of art? So far the western natives have had no education according to our standards but the Finke River mission has been working with them for a number years. Through the efforts of Pastor F. W. Albrecht the western tribes have been kept on the Aboriginal Reserve, although a new home has been found for some of them at Haast Bluff and Areyonga. The Finke River mission is working with them at present and is prepared to carry on in co-operation with the Government. Of course the conditions are different from those at the mission at Hermannsburg, since Haast Bluff and Areyonga are on Government Aboriginal Reserves.

Work is the only salvation of these people. It is to be hoped that the Government will do more than just hand out rations: this makes beggars and loafers, and would mean that the Australian aborigines as a race were doomed. I know the Government means well, but the whole set-up of Government departments tends to kill initiative and independence. Unless the natives have the chance, and are prepared to do something for themselves, their future is hopeless. This is a national affair and it is the Government's duty to see that they are helped to establish themselves as part of our economic system. I believe the only solution is for the Government to co-operate with missions or welfare societies in the task of helping and encouraging these primitive peoples.

Our Australian aborigines have to develop a new race pride if they are going to continue. Before the white man came to this country, the stone-age people lived as a complete organization; otherwise they could not have survived for centuries in their isolation. During that period it was a hard life; but every member of the different tribes knew his duty towards his tribe and his fellow members. This system existed mainly through their marvellous bushcraft and rigid marriage laws. They had absolute faith in their old men to control the elements making rain, to heal the sick, and to re-create people, animals, birds, fish, insects, and plants at will through the performance of their corroboree ceremonies. With the clash of a more modern civilization with its doctors, scientists, and mechanical aids, the young men have lost faith in their elders. Loss of faith has always been more noticeable when they come to our towns and cities, with the result that the tribes break up. The aborigines, their interest in their tribe lost, have no aim in life and no desire to live. If any of the groups of aborigines still in existence and in contact with our more modern civilization are to survive, they must re-create a race pride.

The Negroes in U.S.A. have done this partly through organized sport. Owing to the colour bar they were kept out of white man's society; but by organized sport they have won world recognition which has given their race lustre and their own people pride in themselves.

The art development among the Arunta tribe is the greatest opportunity the Australian aboriginal has had to show the peoples of the world what he is capable of doing. As art speaks all languages, it has given them tremendous prestige; but this prestige is of no use to them as a race unless the aborigines themselves gain race pride through it. I think they have gained much from their art, because over the whole of Australia there seems to be an awakening among them, especially in the field of art. Another noticeable thing is that whereas a few years ago half-caste and quarter-caste aboriginal sportsmen did not want to be called aborigines, now they appear to be proud of the word aboriginal and use it. Among the group of Arunta artists one can see a feeling of pride growing: they want to take a more important part generally, even in the running of the mission at Hermannsburg.

They are also becoming more interested in better housing conditions. Unfortunately it is only a few who are able to afford better living conditions, and even they are handicapped by the terrific drain on their resources by their host of poor relations.

To encourage this race pride before it is too late, organized sport should be encouraged, especially in places like Central Australia, where there are large groups of natives crowded together with very little more to do than collect their rations. Sport could be organized at places such as Hermannsburg, Jay Creek, Alice Springs, Arltunga, Areyonga, Haast Bluff and Yuendoomoo. Teams of athletes, footballers, and players of native games could have competitions against one another. By competition the young men would be trained and encouraged to take an interest in themselves; their cleanliness and appearance would gain thereby. The women would also take more interest in their men, and their tribal groups would gain also. Sport would have a more general influence than art. In districts like Alice Springs pure-blooded aboriginies have had no opportunity to take part in organized sport against white teams because of the feeling against colour; but there is no reason why they should not have competitions among themselves, if the people in control are interested and willing to help.

PLATE I

GHOST GUM, WESTERN MACDONNELLS

ALBERT NAMATJIRA

This water-colour was painted in 1944 near Haast Bluff, which is on the aboriginal reserve about 150 miles west of Alice Springs.

Ghost gums really belong to the mountains, but because this tree is growing in the rich soil of the plains, it has reached giant proportions. The tree with the dark bark is an ironwood. Albert's painting of the shadow on the ghost gum and his treatment of the dry grass in the foreground are masterly.

This water-colour is in the possession of H. R. Balfour, Esq.

PLATE II

MANGERAKA GORGE

ALBERT NAMATJIRA

This water-colour, although painted as early as 1938, already shows a lot of quality and does not lose by its simpler or more primitive handling. It is a remarkable piece of work, considering that Albert had been painting for only two years.

Mangeraka is the aboriginal name of a rock-hole in this gorge which is in the eastern end of Mount Crawford, a flat-topped mountain in the Western Macdonnells, 200 miles west of Alice Springs.

PLATE III

MACDONNELL RANGE

ALBERT NAMATJIRA

This water-colour was painted in 1941 in the Macdonnell Range near Jay Creek, about 30 miles west of Alice Springs. This painting shows Albert in a decorative mood and at his best as a draughtsman and craftsman. It would be difficult to fault this picture.

PLATE IV

SIMPSON'S GAP, MACDONNELL RANGE

ALBERT NAMATJIRA

This water-colour was painted in 1943. Simpson's Gap is one of the most important gaps in the Macdonnell Range and is about fourteen miles west of Alice Springs. This painting is full of quality, especially the shadow on the mountain range.

The drawing and perspective of the foreground plain are remarkable.

PLATE V

MOUNT SONDER, MACDONNELL RANGE

EDWIN PAREROULTJA

This picture, painted on 25th October 1943, is the first water-colour painted on paper by Edwin. Mount Sonder is one of the main landmarks seen from Hermannsburg and is a popular subject with all the aboriginal artists, including Albert Namatjira. On the opposite side of this painting Edwin started his first attempt of the same subject in the manner of Albert Namatjira, but did not finish it, as he decided to discard all thoughts of Albert's work. Albert usually puts in a lion-shaped hill, which is at the right-hand end of this mountain, and Edwin put it in his preliminary sketch; but in this painting he discarded the small hill to show his original sense of decoration. This picture is remarkable for its strong drawing and colouring, although it is really only in three primary colours. A remarkable painting for a first attempt.

PLATE VI

GHOST GUM AND MOUNT SONDER

EDWIN PAREROULTJA

This water-colour was painted by Edwin in 1945. The colouring is softer
and more subtle than in Plate V. The strong point in this picture is Edwin's
aboriginal sense of decoration: even the foliage of the tree is used purely as
decoration to fill a blank corner in the sky. His balance is amazing. This
painting is also a good example of Edwin's colour pattern. His planes are
definite and fit into a natural pattern, and the picture holds its perspective.

PLATE VII

JAMES RANGE

EDWIN PAREROULTJA

This water-colour was painted by Edwin in 1945 in the James Range near Areyonga. The colouring in this picture is like an opal and shows Edwin's wonderful feeling of colour. It is also a good example of his colour pattern and sense of decoration. There are four parallel ranges with a gum-tree creek cutting through them. This picture, as well as being faithfully drawn, is a perfect piece of decoration.

PLATE VIII

MOUNT SONDER FROM ORMISTON GORGE

EDWIN PAREROULTJA

This water-colour was painted in 1946. Edwin has regained the power which he shows in his first painting but with much more quality and colour and more variety in his pattern. It is a brilliant picture and a good example of Edwin's gifts and shows freedom combined with strong drawing.

PLATE IX

HAAST BLUFF, MACDONNELL RANGE

OTTO PAREROULTJA

Painted in the early part of 1946, looking north-west to Haast Bluff in the Western Macdonnells, which is about 160 miles west of Alice Springs. At this stage Otto had a definite style but did not show the rhythm which marks his later pictures.

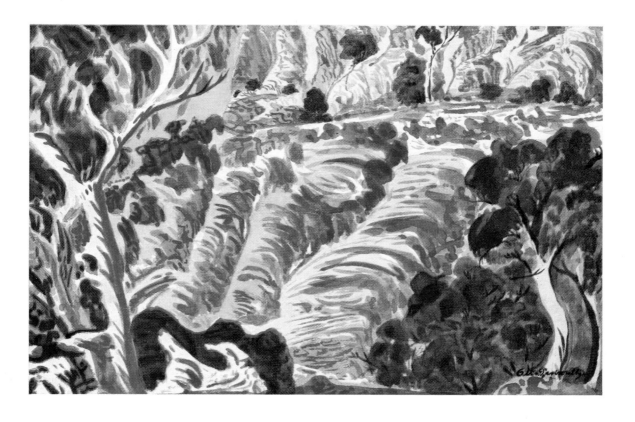

PLATE X

ORMISTON GORGE, MACDONNELL RANGE

OTTO PAREROULTJA

Ormiston Gorge, situated near Mount Giles, is the most remarkable gorge
in Central Australia. This water-colour of the southern wall of the Gorge was
painted by Otto in 1946. Nothing quite like it has ever been painted before. It is
full of rhythm from beginning to end and looks like a piece of tapestry showing
a lot of natural aboriginal quality and decoration.

PLATE XI

ORMISTON GORGE

OTTO PAREROULTJA

Painted in 1946, a few days later than Plate X, this remarkable picture gives a very good idea of Ormiston Gorge and is faithful in both drawing and colour with that extra quality of rhythm which Otto possesses. It almost looks like a fire with the near rock wall red-hot and the far wall a moving mass of flames and smoke. Even the foliage of the ghost gum is caught up in the flame effect. The whole picture is a beautiful decoration and, like this unspoilt artist, is perfectly natural.

PLATE XII

GUM-TREE AND GORGE, JAMES RANGE

OTTO PAREROULTJA

Otto painted this picture in 1948. It is full of rhythm and it is a true presentation of this rugged country. It also shows Otto's later development, in which he has unconsciously gone back into his own tribal mythology and used its symbolism of circles and wavy lines like those used in the drawings on the sacred churungas of the Arunta tribe.

PLATE XIII

VALLEY, JAMES RANGE

REUBEN PAREROULTJA

Painted in 1945, this work reveals the refined and delicate nature of the
artist. It is beautifully drawn, especially the perspective of the trees growing in the
creek. The pale yellow colouring on the hills is of the dry spinifex or porcupine
grass.

PLATE XIV

ORMISTON GORGE, MACDONNELL RANGE

REUBEN PAREROULTJA

This decorative, mural-like water-colour was painted by Reuben in 1946 and shows his wonderful natural sense of decoration. The picture is true to nature; the blue rocks in the foreground are in the bed of the Ormiston Creek, as are the two river gums, while the background is composed of two rock walls, the far wall being about 900 feet high.

PLATE XV

FINKE RIVER BANK, MACDONNELL RANGE

WALTER EBATARINJA

Painted in the Finke River Gorge at Glen Helen in 1945. This water-colour shows the tremendous influence Albert Namatjira had on Walter Ebatarinja's work at that time, especially in his outlook, colouring, and in the treatment of his trees. It is a fine water-colour and, although lacking the originality of Walter's later work, it shows a lot of quality and technical ability.

PLATE XVI

RIVER GUM, MACDONNELL RANGE

ENOS NAMATJIRA

Painted at Glen Helen in 1945 by Albert Namatjira's eldest son, Enos. This well-composed water-colour shows that Enos has been influenced by his father in outlook, although it shows a greater preference for strong purples than do his father's paintings. Enos still favours purple in his later work but has developed a keener sense of decoration.

PLATE XVII

GHOST GUM, ROMA, MACDONNELL RANGE

OSKAR NAMATJIRA

A water-colour painted in 1948 by Oskar at Roma, which is situated on the north-west boundary of the Hermannsburg country and is about 25 miles from the mission station. In this picture Oskar still shows some of the influence of his father Albert Namatjira, but there is more strength and a greater feeling for decoration than in his earlier work.

The water-colour is in the possession of A. P. Latz, Esq.

PLATE XVIII

A JAMES RANGE GORGE

HENOCH RABERABA

Henoch had only been painting in water-colours for two years when he painted this brilliant picture in 1948. The sense of decoration, good drawing, strong light, beautiful colour harmony, and free handling are amazing for any artist, let alone one who had been painting for such a short time.

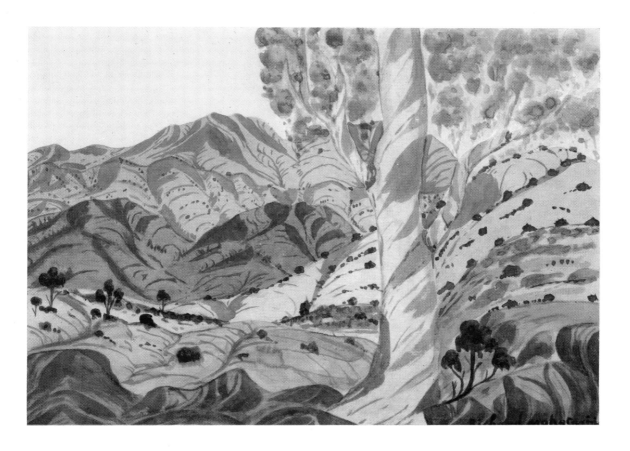

PLATE XIX

MOUNT GILES, MACDONNELL RANGE

RICHARD MOKETARINJA

This water-colour was painted in the early part of 1948 and shows the strong originality of Richard, also his primitive sense of decoration. The colour is good; but his drawing is one of his outstanding qualities. The flatness of the gum-tree helps his decoration because it forms part of the picture and does not become just a portrait.

PLATE XX

PALM VALLEY, JAMES RANGE

RICHARD MOKETARINJA

Painted in October 1948. This powerful piece of decoration shows the strong personality of Richard Moketarinja, who appears to be the most primitive of the group. This picture portrays the wild ruggedness and colour of Palm Valley with strong drawing and strong contrasts in textures and forms.

PLATE XXI

RAIN, JAMES RANGE

EWALD NAMATJIRA

Painted in 1948 by Albert Namatjira's third artist son. The rarity of rain in Central Australia makes it particularly interesting to the aboriginals and rain is one of Ewald Namatjira's favourite subjects. This water-colour shows his remarkable powers of observation, as he has caught the whole atmosphere and feeling of moisture on the hills as the sun shines through the clouds. The drawing is excellent, especially of the ironwood-tree.